MASTERING SMALL BUSINESS EMPLOYEE ENGAGEMENT

30 Quick Wins & HR Hacks from an IIP Platinum Employer

JAYNE GALLAGHER, MD
BARRY PHILLIPS, CEO

Matador
9 Priory Business Park,
Wistow Road, Kibworth Beauchamp,
Leicestershire. LE8 0RX
Tel: 0116 279 2299
Email: books@troubador.co.uk
Web: www.troubador.co.uk/matador
Twitter: @matadorbooks

ISBN 978 183859 354 4

British Library Cataloguing in Publication Data.
A catalogue record for this book is available from the British Library.

Printed and bound by CPI Group (UK) Ltd, Croydon, CR0 4YY
Typeset in 11pt Minion Pro by Troubador Publishing Ltd, Leicester, UK

Matador is an imprint of Troubador Publishing Ltd

Barry Phillips
BEM, CEO, Legal Island

Barry Phillips is founder and CEO of Legal Island a multi award winning training and compliance company in the UK and Ireland. He was awarded a BEM in the 2020 New Year's Honours List for services to employment and equality.

A qualified barrister, mediator, and coach he is a speaker both nationally and internationally. He has multiple business interests and directorships. Currently, he mentors several SMEs in the UK and abroad.

He's an Ironman and married with a daughter, rating Russian language and literature and wild camping as his favourite pastimes.

Jayne Gallagher
Managing Director, Legal Island

Responsible for the day to day running and management of the company and employees, Jayne's experience in people management spans 15 years.

A business studies graduate and qualified Chartered Marketer, Jayne is a TedX speaker, mentor and coach. She sits on numerous charitable boards including Orchardville and the Cancer Research UK Business Beats Cancer, Belfast.

Currently, Jayne and her husband, Allen, are busy looking after their first baby, Henry, a new arrival for 2020.

To our dear friend the late Richard O'Rawe
Business scholar, coach, gentleman.

CONTENTS

PREFACE

Barry Phillips, Founder and CEO of Legal Island

When I started Legal Island in 1998 I thought I knew everything there was to know about running a business and managing people. I mean, how difficult could it be? I had been working as a practising employment lawyer. I had written and published material on employment issues. I fully understood the parameters of employing a person and to boot I had just completed an MBA at the University of Ulster. In short, I was set up to be the perfect business leader... wasn't I?

In truth, the first three, maybe four years, proved to be a long, slow and very cold bath...

Whilst training as a barrister in London I was always keen to make an impression and share my insights. I once offered to a senior barrister in chambers what I thought then was a great idea for service improvement. Of course, it would have required changes to many procedures but the benefits would have been huge. To this day some 25 years on I can still hear his reply in my head and word for word too: "My dear boy we've been doing things like this perfectly well for the past 300 years. Why on earth would we want to change now?"!

It was this, together with other incidents too, that convinced me I was in the wrong profession and if ever I had a go at running my own business I'd aim to make it as "unlawyerlike" as possible.

Perhaps subconsciously that was how I set about building my company Legal Island. For the first few years I kept true to my promise. I always liked and followed the well used ethos of work hard, party hard. And boy did we party! I took my staff karting and hot air ballooning. We flew abroad for team building weekends and spent a Christmas Party in Riga Latvia dressed in medieval costume.

We were having a great time – or so I thought. Then one day, a staff member unexpectedly handed in her notice. "Hah! Can't take the pace," I thought. "Probably better off gone." Then a second, a third and a fourth employee left in as many weeks. Four may not sound alarming to you but at the time I had just 12 employees and this amounted to a sizeable chunk of the workforce gone almost overnight. Ask yourself, could your business take a hit of that magnitude without you wobbling?

What disturbed me most was that those leaving were none too complimentary about their time in the company. They pointed to failing systems (or complete lack thereof), a lack of vision "from the top" (yes me...!) and difficult working relations. This kind of feedback was hard to take but it's compounded when it comes from family. Let me explain, this last statement.

When you begin a business from the ground up and start to take on employees it does feel like you are part of, and indeed head of, a family – at times it can feel more like a family than it does a commercial enterprise. Like it or not, as the founder of a small business, you're right in amongst everyone from the very start. You give some people what might be their first ever job, a foot onto the working ladder. You give others their first experience of a career that they realise might prove to be their lifetime vocation. You wish staff a great weekend as they leave on Friday afternoons and welcome them back on Monday. Over lunch you hear their stories, you find out about their own worlds. You help them by being as flexible as you dare allow in terms of working hours and time off. You drop them off to dental appointments, give them added time off for family occasions. You believe in them. Invest in them. And then, sometimes without warning, they leave. You peer at a gaping hole and you're left to re-shape the "family unit" all over again.

Looking back on the "deluge" of resignations presented to me I guess I was left dazed. The guy on paper (me) who could make it look so easy was finding it impossibly hard. But I never thought nor wanted to give up on my company. I was in this far and in too deep to quit. I had risked money, time and my own reputation. I simply had to make this work. It wasn't a difficult choice because there was no choice. It was forwards or fail. There was no other path.

My response was to call in the very first of many outside consultants that we were to use to grow Legal Island and indeed transform the company. Her name was Fiona Keenan. My brief to her was simple. Tell me what I'm doing wrong. Tell me straight, then help me fix it.

You might say there were no surprises in her report to me when it arrived the following week. Certainly, now looking back it all seems so clear but you know what they say about hindsight – and it's all too true. In short, she advised me that I was trying to run before I had learnt to walk. It was okay to play she said and play hard but only when you've first dropped in basic people management procedures to help the business run smoothly. Each mention she made of any process came at me from her like a blow to the head. The woman I was paying a lot of money to was sitting in front of me advising me to take a road that hitherto I had avoided because it just wasn't exciting enough. In fact, I knew it would bore me to death. A range of emotions then splurged out – anger, frustration and I guess, relief too, for I knew she was right.

Cleverly, Fiona suggested that we aim for Investors in People (IIP) accreditation. Smart move Fiona. She knew I liked goals and something to aim for and our first badge might comfort the pain that was to come as we straightened everything out. And so began our journey towards IIP Platinum.

Fiona had also helped me realise too who I was and where my skills set lay. This was something I had overlooked at the start. Yet another obvious exercise to do – completely missed. I was the vision person. I was the guy who saw the big picture. What I needed was the people to make it work and the resources to pull it together.

I urgently needed someone who was a completer/finisher – the implementer for Legal Island. Someone who could take the baton from me sometimes walking, sometimes running, and get us across the finish line. Unbeknown to me I had already found her...

Jayne Gallagher MD

When I joined Legal Island in 2007 I hadn't really given much thought to the future. I was 26 and had just returned to Belfast from Glasgow having completed a maternity cover contract in an event management role in a large corporate organisation. Now home, my only thoughts were immediate and centred around how quickly I could buy myself somewhere to live and where would my next holiday with friends take me. Holidays I had thought of but truth be told, I hadn't a clue where my next job would take me.

My path into event management started when, having finished University with no clear direction of the career I wanted to take, (the popular journey across the water into consultancy firms didn't appeal to me and in my heart of hearts I knew I was a home bird), I had to ask myself the question of "what was I really good at?".

Being organised is something I've always had a thing about, my school and university diaries were meticulous.

I enjoyed organising get-togethers, being the hostess and I was never late for anything. So recognising this as a skill, I set about putting organisation into a career and looked in the direction of event management.

After building up a few years' management experience and a stint in Glasgow, I started with Legal Island as the Events Manager for Ireland. This was a job that involved travel and long hours and suited me down to the ground. I had no commitments and event management had been my career for the last three years so I was comfortable and confident in the role. What followed, however, was a career path I didn't expect.

I became part of the company growth plan for the next few years. I got involved in strategy, I understood what Barry was trying to achieve and, importantly, I think I understood Barry, the boss. What I didn't understand or realise I was good at was working with and managing people, and it took Barry to point it out to me.

About five years into the role, Barry, said to me "want to be MD? I think you'd be quite good at it".

Something I've discovered I tend to do is say yes to nearly every opportunity presented to me. I'm no adrenaline junkie so to be clear saying yes to opportunities doesn't mean I'll say yes when asked to swim the River Lagan (I'm a useless swimmer) or to sing solo in front of a crowd (never ask me to hold a note), but ask me to join a committee or Board or speak at a public event, I'll likely get quickly bought into the idea and say yes, thinking about the longer term consequences after. The truth is, when someone has faith in you and believes in your ability to take on a job or a responsibility, it's difficult to not get bought into their enthusiasm and their belief in you – to ultimately feel empowered. So, I said yes to MD.

What followed was nine years of learning and growing – not just for the company but also for myself. I discovered tools and practices I'd not engaged with before that made a phenomenal difference. I cannot speak more highly of the use of coaches and mentors – the difference these people made to me has been incredible. I had to make difficult decisions and have difficult conversations as well as have the pleasure of giving some great news about company and staff developments.

And so, what was started by Barry, on a loan from a family member of a few hundred pounds, became and is now a business with 25 staff, turning over close on £2million and puts its people at its core. And it's been one hell of a journey to this point. Nine years after Barry gave me the push I didn't even know I needed, I am proud to be the MD of Legal Island.

But best of all? In this time we've seen employees grow and develop beyond all recognition. Some have stayed and are now key employees doing leading edge work while others have left spring boarding from us to dizzy heights far on the horizon.

Between Barry and I we hope to share with you the things we do that help us secure good engagement with our people. We genuinely believe that people have a right to get up and go to work in an environment in which they can flourish. This is our small contribution to making that happen...

PROLOGUE

Barry Phillips

If you've purchased this book to find out more about employee engagement you're invited to skip this Prologue. However, if this much is true but you're also a business owner you may wish to continue reading. What I share here are my reflections on developing a start-up, finding yourself as an entrepreneur and the challenges you face devising and rolling out new products and services.

Before the Beginning

You might say that the genesis of Legal Island can be traced back to 1976 when, at the age of just 11, I got my first ever paid job working as a paper delivery boy. I had called the local newsagent where I lived in Ottery St Mary, Devon, and the proprietor showed up at our house in his super-fast sports car. The interview, if that's what you could call it, took place at my garden gate. When he asked me if my dad was okay about me working early in the morning, I told him that he was at sea at present (he had returned to the merchant navy for a while after being made redundant) and that he didn't know I was applying for my first job, but my mum was okay with it. I guess I thought he might take pity on a fatherless boy and this would be reflected in my wages. Looking back on it now, I think my plan backfired. Instead, he probably thought he could pay this boy very little without ever having to deal with an irate father. He paid me £1.90 a week which in today's money equates to just £15.18p. Bear in mind that this was for a paper round that took me an hour to complete every day and two hours on Sundays, when the papers were also twice as heavy with so many supplements. Oddly, but perhaps fittingly, my calculator tells me that, when rounded up, this equates to £1.90 per hour in today's money.

After almost two years of delivering in all weather and road conditions, I decided to ask for a pay rise. I determined that if I opened the negotiations at £2.50, my employer might counter at £2 and I'd then offer to meet him halfway at £2.25. I opened. He didn't counter. Instead, he sacked me.

For days afterwards, I reflected on the injustice of it all. I wondered whether the other paper boys would rally behind me, and whether I could persuade them to withdraw their labour until I was re-instated. But they were too dispersed, too glad of any money to risk their own and in truth, I didn't carry enough clout to lead them into this sort of workers' uprising anyway. After all, Devon was the kind of place where nothing much ever happened, least of all an uprising of paper boys who weren't delivering the *Daily Telegraph* to the well-healed and well retired in time for breakfast.

But it did cause me to think about unequal bargaining powers and the absence of laws to make things fairer. I became curious to know why there was no law requiring this man to pay me a decent wage. At the time, the only law that appeared relevant was one making employment of anyone under 13 illegal; and my employer was even breaking that.

Anyway, this early interest in justice and law stayed with me for many years, leading me to do a degree in law at university.

Legal Island – The Beginning

Fast forward to 1995; I had qualified as a barrister and had moved to Northern Ireland to specialise in employment law.

Early on, working as an employment specialist, I realised that the only way to keep up to date on employment law developments was to fly to an annual update conference in London every year. I noticed that there were a good number of us from Northern Ireland who attended. In those days, pre the advent of budget airlines, the cost of a flight to London from Belfast was a good £200. By the time you had paid for the event, a night in a hotel (if you decided to go the night before), then trains and taxis, you (or your employer) were out of pocket to the tune of around £700.

The other drawback was that no one at this conference explained the differences between the law in England and

Wales, and in Northern Ireland. So, as I was flying home one evening, I thought, 'Why not organise an event in Belfast?' My plan was to use local solicitors and barristers and charge an entry fee which would be a fraction of the cost of a trip to London.

I ran the idea past a few friends and was warned firmly against it. One said that if it was an idea with legs, it would have been done by now. An observation that had some merit I suppose, but it was ultimately a view that amounted to never doing anything that's new and untried. Another friend advised me to steer well clear of a world of which I had no experience, namely business and entrepreneurship. A third, who I now know to be something of a doom monger, immediately pointed to the embarrassment I would feel amongst my peers when I had invited lots of successful lawyers to speak to an audience of what could turn out to be just a few people.

Needless to say, I ignored all of this advice and went ahead and set up a company that today has a turnover approaching £2million. It gives truly meaningful employment to twenty-five staff and delivers what I believe to be really great service.

Thanks for the advice, but...

Knowing when to act on advice and when not to is probably one of the hardest skills in business. It really is so difficult. In attempting to filter out good from bad advice, you can do a number of things. You can ask yourself whether the person offering the advice has any direct experience of the type of issue you want help with – and discount it if he or she hasn't. You can also discount the advice if you know the person may have an ulterior motive for advising you one way or the other, but you're then running the risk of excluding advice that could be well-meant and really on the money. Also, you can fall into the trap of over-asking, leaving yourself with too many viewpoints to consider. Then, add to this the danger of over thinking. Academics, they say, are lousy at running universities because they spend far too much time analysing their next move and overthinking each step.

What's interesting now, however, is that I never asked the main questions that I should have posed myself right at the beginning, and they are:

- Am I an entrepreneur?
- Is this what I'm good at?
- Do I have the skillset to develop my own business and the self-awareness to know what I'm good at?
- Do I know what I'll have to outsource or delegate quickly, once the juggernaut starts moving?

When I look back now, there were many indications that I had an entrepreneur within me, but it's interesting that I never paused for one moment to ask myself these questions. As a young boy, I was always wheeling and dealing in the playground selling pencils and fancy pens. Then, as a teenager, the merchandise matured to cigarettes and magazines that were best kept hidden from teachers and parents. At university, I was forever organising people and giving them things to do or try: barn dances, parachute jumps, ice-skating trips or weekends in Paris.

Roll Out of Service One:
Legal Information and Training Events

So, one morning in about July 1998, I decided to organise the first annual conference for Northern Ireland on employment law developments. I sought the help of a barrister friend of mine who specialised in employment law; he remains a friend to this day, and a shareholder in the company.

I went to the Belfast Library, got out the Yellow Pages and took a note of every organisation that was big enough to be able to pay for a half-page advert. My reasoning was that if they had the resources to do that, they'd also have the resources to attend my event aimed at human resources managers and have the money to pay for it.

I knocked up a one-page flyer (which I still have to this day) and a covering letter, simply addressed to the HR manager. I bought some three hundred second class stamps and as many A5 envelopes, and I spent the best part of a weekend addressing them by hand before putting them in the post. I remember that, rather than posting them all at once, I chose to post 50 per day for almost a week, in a different post box each time. I figured that if they went out on the same day from one box, I was risking the whole venture. What if someone set fire to its contents overnight, or the postman drove into the river and drowned the next day, along with all my flyers? It was day one and I was already thinking about worse-case scenarios, learning to spread my risk and, you might think, cope with a good deal of early paranoia.

With six weeks to go to the big day, I still had not landed a single customer. But then, shortly afterwards, an envelope appeared with half of my flyer returned and completed. But best of all, there was my first cheque for £145 and one place at the event. It was from one of the Health Boards – one of Northern Ireland's biggest employers. I thought, 'Wow!' If they believed in it, surely others would too? With four weeks to go, five people had booked. It was much better than one, but still barely enough to cover the hotel deposit (which they were insisting was overdue). Two weeks later, 11 had booked. With one week to go, it was 26. Finally, D-Day arrived: 32 people.

I remember the day very well. We had some top-line speakers, including one of the best employment lawyers in the business in Northern Ireland, Beverley Jones. At the time, microfiches were all the rage and I had borrowed a projector from the hotel which had clearly seen better days. When Beverley was speaking, she asked me to change the acetates. I sat next to the overhead projector and noticed that it was beginning to overheat. Smoke was coming out the back. I fanned it as best I could without distracting Beverley and drawing delegates' attention to just how little money had been spent on equipment for this first event.

So, that was the end of the first day's trading and I had made enough money to pay for the hotel and the speakers, while rolling some profit forward.

The Name "Legal Island" and this "Internet Thing"

People have asked where the name Legal Island came from and I wish I could say that it came about after a lot of market research and consultation with a good few branding experts, but this would be far from the truth.

Just before the first conference, I was messing about on my PC having just purchased a magazine all about this new thing called "The Internet". On the front page, the magazine was promising readers that it could show you how to get a web page published using the floppy disk that came free inside. After a couple of hours playing around, I had managed to do two pages and by joining them together, I had created what was, in effect, a very basic website with links to other sites that I thought might be of interest to those involved in HR. One of those pages was relevant to those working in Northern Ireland, the other for those in the Republic of Ireland. After two hours of playing, I wasn't really sure if I had anything worth saving, but I was asked for a file name to drop onto the floppy disk. It was legal and it was to do with our island, so I called the file "Legal Island". That's how the name came about.

That "Internet thing" proved critical to the early development of Legal Island for two reasons. Firstly, it offered me a way to structure the company and grow it at little cost. Secondly, it provided me with a second income stream at just the right time.

Whilst my opening business salvo had been a success, the few hundred quid profit made wasn't enough to justify the rental of an office or hiring core staff. So, for the first few years of Legal Island's precarious life, I recruited only home workers. I set each of them up with a PC, Internet and phone connection. It suited them as most were working mothers with duties to do before logging in at 9am, and it suited me because it effectively meant I didn't need any bricks and mortar – an overhead which might have wiped us out at that early point. I was doing the same too; working from home. At one point, the joke was that I had the shortest commuting distance of any worker. My office was also my bedroom. At night, the sofa in my office/bedroom would pull out into a bed. When I awoke in the morning, I could press the start button of the PC with my foot hanging over the edge of the bed. I was then effectively at work.

Roll Out of Service Two:
Weekly Employment Law Updates by Email

The other reason the internet proved so important to the development of the company was because it gave us an important second income stream at a very early stage. Of course, it didn't only give us web pages, but also this other thing called "email," which was still only known to a few people.

Sometime in 1998, I figured that it would be worth starting a weekly review of employment law developments specific to Northern Ireland that I would send out to people via this medium called "email". After 12 months of doing this, I had just 10 subscribers. Ok, they were paying £85 a year to receive the emails, but writing reviews of new case law and legislation was time consuming and at these figures, it wasn't worth the candle. But then something happened. Everyone seemed to get email at once. I had clearly got in just at the right time. By year two, 100 people had subscribed, by year three it was 400, and by year four, I had over 600 subscribers.

A big consideration in business is when to move forward with something that you see is going to disrupt the market. The answer is not always to go first and get first mover advantage. Remember, the second mouse is the one that gets the cheese. Many early developers of online shopping learnt this to their cost. Early adventurers were badly burned because they had moved when the technology wasn't quite sufficiently developed.

But it seems that I had caught the wave just right. Not only were the numbers going sky high, the marvellous thing was that every additional subscriber was pure profit. There was no extra cost of slipping them onto the email service, other than the admin cost of processing their fees and adding their email addresses to the database.

The Big Roll Out – More than
a Whimper Less than a Roar..

My big mistake, however, was not to roll out a similar service in Britain, where the potential number of subscribers was huge. What I should have done was purchase the names and addresses of the top 10,000 employers in the UK and sent them all a brochure informing them of this brand-new service fronted by a few employment lawyers I still knew from my days at the London Bar. That was my first big mistake. A second blow to the roll out of the email service was probably just as disappointing, although this time it was events that conspired against me rather than my own stupidity.

In year two of the email service, a lawyer and fan of the service who was working for a very large legal support company, approached me and suggested that I should offer it to their company in Britain for them to repackage and sell as their own to their clients. Same cornflakes, different packaging – that sort of thing. He said he didn't have the authority in the company to set up the deal, but he could set up a meeting with the three relevant people who would make the call. I knew this was going to be a big meeting. I figured that their client base had to consist of at least 1,000 companies. Even at a special knock-down rate of £50 per head, I knew this was a lot of money.

I must have spent a week prepping for the meeting, working on figures and making sure I had the information at hand to cover off any queries they might have. At the meeting, they disclosed that their client base was actually nearer 10,000 clients rather than 1,000, and when they didn't baulk at my opening offer of £50 per client, I spent the rest of the meeting trying not to break out in a cold sweat as I saw the pound signs spinning round in my eyes.

For days after the meeting, which seemed to have gone really well, I tried my hardest not to think too far ahead or even mentally consider that the deal was in the bag, but try as I might, I had already purchased the yacht and the fancy car, and was visualising all the trappings that are often said to go with them. A week went by, then two, then three without any news. 'What should I do?' I thought. If I phoned, it might look like I was too keen. I'd left the meeting gently hinting that others were interested in the email service too. Then, after a month, I heard from my lawyer friend with the inside information. It was a complete disaster and shock. The three who had met me, and who would have taken the deal into the company, had left to set up their own organisation in direct competition with their former employer. Everything they had been doing and advocating for had been contaminated by their troubled exit from the company. It was clear that the fancy car and the yacht were going to have to wait. Come to think of it, I'm still waiting.

I did roll out the email service in the Republic of Ireland, however, with huge success and I took the opportunity to improve how we produced it too. Instead of writing it in-house, we got others to do it for us and this is still how it's done today. It's written mainly by solicitors and barristers specialising in employment law, who, through us have an opportunity to get their work and name in front of a lot of potential customers.

Since we started the email service, many law firms have offered email update services of their own – and for free too. But none have got any real traction, and to this day we have no main competitor in this space. The lesson? First mover advantage proved crucial here.

Roll Out of Service Three: E-learning

The third and final main income stream for the company came some ten years later than that of their two earlier siblings: e-learning.

I had thought for a long time that many employers were not doing equality and diversity training and leaving themselves very exposed to costly litigation because of it. As a former lawyer who used to stick claims for harassment on employers and find it too easy to do so, I could never understand why they would expose themselves to a penalty kick without so much as a goalkeeper in front of goal. In short, whenever an employee sues claiming harassment, it is never enough for an employer to show that they responded promptly and fairly as soon as the harassment came to their attention. They have to show that they did all they reasonably could do to prevent the harassment taking place in the first instance.

This is best done by showing three things. Firstly, that you have an equal opportunities policy; secondly, that it has been implemented and thirdly, that equality training has taken place for all staff – not just senior employees. The first two are easy enough to do with the right advice. Logistically, however, the third can be difficult. This is the case because with conventional training it can be difficult to get good availability from a trainer who is much in demand. Getting everyone together on a date that suits her or him can be challenging too, particularly in cases where an employer has multiple sites or employees that spend a lot of time out of the office, whether on the road or abroad.

The solution was not only to provide quality training but to deliver it in a way that would be convenient to the purchaser rather than the deliverer. E-learning had been around for a while – Legal Island certainly didn't invent it. But what we did invent was an e-learning product that was bespoked to Northern Ireland and perfectly positioned to help an employer point to meaningful training in defending liability for a workplace equality issue.

Developing the Product – from Antrim to India

So, how did we go about developing the product from scratch? The first thing I did was to give the development project a very generic name. I think I called it something like the "Chitty Chitty Bang Bang Project". I've always liked how Caracticus Potts wheeled a beaten-up old car that was destined for the scrap heap into the shed. For days, his children wondered what was being created behind closed doors accompanied by so much banging, crashing and cursing. Then, he wheels out a magical product the likes of which had never been seen before. Over time, I've realised that even the name you give a product development assignment can shape it at an early stage and not always for the better. Give an R&D project a very specific label at the start and you risk unduly restricting the direction in which it will be developed and also the ideas others may have for it.

At the time, I had just joined an Invest NI course to assist business leaders with the development of new products. This proved invaluable because it provided me with access to an entrepreneur with direct experience of product development in the IT space; a man by the name of Martin McKay, who was one of the founders of TextHelp, based in Antrim. His initial advice was pivotal in telling me what formats I should consider for my e-learning modules. At the time, 3D animation products seemed to be the next big thing and I was keen to get in early and catch the wave at just the right time. Very helpfully, he set me straight quickly by pointing out two key things:

1. User technology just wasn't ready for 3-D (and it still isn't, incidentally) and that my product had to be cross-platform compatible. In other words, it had to be user-friendly and accessible to as many potential customers as possible
2. All the most popular cartoons in the world are two 2D, not 3; from Tom and Jerry, right through to the Simpsons.

It's interesting that very often, you can access an external resource and ask yourself how much further you got along the journey as a result of doing so. But often, the value to be found is from being saved from making expensive and time-consuming mistakes.

Another early activity in the shed (so to speak) was to look at existing e-learning products. The first I saw was so bad that it almost deterred me from thinking about producing an e-learning product at all. It was well-produced but had far too much content and music playing in the background – presumably to stop the user falling asleep, so bad was its ability to engage the user. It amounted to little more than an online PowerPoint presentation.

But then I found a great example of e-learning made by a firm in the Far East. It had been produced on a minimal budget, but somehow it was very engaging and stood out clearly as I tried one product after another. I showed it to a few colleagues, who agreed it was good. Then, I set about asking myself why, determined to be sure to import the magical ingredients into our own product. I then sourced a company in India with the expertise to develop the product at a very reasonable cost and quickly set about finding a second, in the event that the first relationship didn't work out.

A Minimum Viable Product (MVP)?

A big decision when developing a new product or service is to decide at what point you have something good enough to sell. Any well-regarded manufacturer will tell you that you must never wait until you consider that you have a perfect product before taking it to market. But when do you know you have a minimum viable product that's good enough to at least start bringing in some revenue? I was proud of our first product, but looking back at it now, it appears crude and I'm glad its content dated, and we had to replace it with something more up-to-date. I try to look at these changed feelings as a sign of progress. I say to managers here at Legal Island, 'If you're not thoroughly embarrassed about the manager you were five years ago, you're not developing quickly enough'.

The module or package we eventually offered to the marketplace came with its own web portal. The HR or training officer could see an overview of the portal and track user activity in an instant. Not only could an employer see whether an employee had done the training, they could check to see whether they had understood it and passed the online assessment. Within no time, this module was flying off the shelves, as were others on child protection in schools, and data protection following GDPR. What we had done from the start, we were still doing. We'd test it in Northern Ireland; if it worked here, we'd roll it out in the Republic of Ireland and sometimes in Britain too.

Other Services and Entrepreneurial Activities

There were other products I developed as well. I wrote and marketed an e-book on how to make and deliver a best man's speech. I developed an online application to help business leaders understand how to use Twitter for their own branding and business marketing. Both sold, but the returns were too low to justify more time marketing either of them. Since starting Legal Island, I have owned a property investment company, partnered with a charity to set up a pop up restaurant and recently set up a luxury travel business.

Some business initiatives will work, some will not. There's a great skill in knowing when to persevere with a new idea and when to abandon it. Undoubtedly, I've held on to ideas for too long in the past that, in hindsight, were destined to fail. But it is easy to be wise after the event. What I do know is that you have be prepared to fail. Vulnerability is part of being an entrepreneur and a leader. If you don't have it in a company, you won't achieve the right levels of creativity and innovation in the first place.

INTRODUCTION

Mind the Gap – the Engagement Gap

*To win in the marketplace you
must first win in the workplace.*
Doug Conant[1]

Ask yourself this question:

*Is it the employers' duty to save us all from
boredom and workplace disillusionment?*

According to a recent survey as many as 85% of employees are not engaged in the workplace[2]. Worse still, some of these employees are *actively disengaged* – in other words actively working against the interests of their employer. That's a lot of people getting up every day going to work unhappy or with a very dubious mission plan. Equally, that's a lot of an employer's time devoted to turning

---

1   Former CEO, Campbell Soup Company and Founder/CEO,
     ConantLeadership.
2   State of the Global Workplace 2017 https://www.gallup.com/
     services/178517/state-global-workplace.aspx

around negative aspects of a business and diverting them from front end productivity.

Adam Smith may be said to be the founder of the boring job when he advocated division of labour principles as far back as the 1700s. He acknowledged that early forms of assembly line production weren't at all motivating but he also believed that many people didn't like work and it didn't matter to them anyway.

Some 300 years on, not only we have moved on from a predominantly manufacture based economy, but thankfully, we have also moved on from the belief that we shouldn't expect to go to work to feel valued and stimulated by the work we do.

So, then ask yourself this question.

Is it an employer's duty to try
to make employees happy?

We think not.

OK, how about this:

Is it their duty to create an environment in
which employees can be happy and thrive?

We think yes.

Let's not forget though, that this engagement thing is a two-way process. It requires thought, input and activity from employees as well as the small employer. As one business leader said to us recently with a hint of sarcasm there's only so long an employer can do this engagement thing on their own.

Be under no misunderstanding, however. You can't buy engagement. You can throw all the money you like at an employee by uplifting salary 20% or by handing out a generous bonus just in time for Christmas. Their motivation and commitment at work may improve but it will be both slight and temporary.

Conversely, poor remuneration is demotivating, and you can do all the work you like in other areas that normally engage staff to little effect.

So, remuneration for us belongs in a separate category standing aside from other factors that drive engagement. But it's not out there on its own.

We believe it works in partnership with another "must have" element – wellbeing and the working environment.

Unless an employee's place of work is conducive to healthy thinking, reflection and positive output he or she will quickly slip down the continuum that is marked "actively disengaged" at one end and "highly engaged" at the other.

So, it's about two plus six. The critical two – remuneration and wellbeing – and then the big six.

Many metaphors jump to mind but the xylophone with six notes played by two mallets is probably our favourite. When the two mallets are working well across the six notes great melodies result.

3

The other six are:

- Values, Vision, Mission and Employee Values
- Job Design
- Recognition
- Learning & Development
- Communication – Interpersonal and Internal
- Leadership

Maybe there's a corny acronym waiting to be had here to help us remember these six. But we think time is better spent working on how to apply them – an altogether more demanding exercise.

This book takes you through all of these as clearly and as simply as our writing skills allow. As we do so we identify areas for quick wins and for competitive advantage because at the end of the day having employees coming to work (and indeed leaving) all pumped up is commendable, but strong bottom line figures are the best guarantee that your staff engagement strategy is working and deserves to stay – albeit as an evolving process.

CHAPTER ONE

Remuneration

The King gave orders that the page's salary was to be doubled. As he received no salary at all this was not of much use to him, but it was considered a great honour, and was duly published in the Court Gazette.
Oscar Wilde

Key Observations

- Remunerating staff fairly is one of the toughest challenges you face in an SME – it is essential that you ring-fence adequate time and resource to do it well
- It is important to remember that salary is an inefficient way of remunerating staff – think instead in terms of benefits you can pass on to your employees
- Incentivising staff by direct performance-related pay is difficult to do – you should do this with care or avoid it altogether
- Don't forget to remind staff of the benefits you give them – they may think the grass is greener elsewhere if you don't point out the green grass around their feet

Introduction

Money hey? Pah! Who needs it? The truth is we all do. Strange then, perhaps, that in an interview you can never admit, even in part, that you're there for the money.

Money, much maligned as the root of all evil, takes care of the weekly shopping, the monthly utility bills, the annual holidays and a pension pot for a happy retirement. It provides security and allows individuals to plan for the future. These may be big plans too, such as getting a mortgage, a first house, starting a family. Make no mistake, what you decide to pay a person will determine who will apply for a post and possibly how long they will stay. But will it have a bearing on the level of engagement you can expect? Now that's a million-dollar question. Ah ... we're back to money again.

In the introduction to this book we stuck our necks out and said that you can't buy engagement simply by throwing money at employees. But we also said that you must remunerate fairly to have any real expectation of creating a workplace in which you can begin to achieve levels of engagement that will give you competitive advantage. You see, what you pay your staff has a direct bearing on both value and trust. People assess their own worth, at least in part, by the size of their pay packet. Underpaid employees will feel undervalued by you their employer, the one who is out to maximise their engagement and value. It's as simple as that.

Trust also becomes an issue. If employees take the view that their employer is unable or unwilling to assess and pay the current market rate for their post, they may not trust you to make the other big business calls. That is why remuneration, i.e. pay plus all the other benefits for working somewhere, is one item, along with wellbeing that must always exist for an SME employer to have any chance of achieving healthy levels of engagement. Remember, we call these the Critical Two. With the other six areas we will cover, you are afforded some leeway. You could get one or more slightly wrong or even badly wrong and you may still have a chance of securing reasonable levels of engagement. Not so with remuneration and wellbeing.

The next chapter looks at wellbeing, but for now let's focus on remuneration, where we've got good news and bad. The good is that we believe remuneration presents SMEs with great opportunities for stealing a march on competitors, that's if it's done well. The bad news is that this is a complex topic and you'll really have to work to earn your place ahead of the field.

A good payment strategy requires you to know market rates, be cognisant of internal relationships, and to watch cash flows and profit projections closely. Occasionally, to make the right appointment you have to pay a salary that you know you can afford only if your profit projections are right. That's risky ... welcome to the world of running a business.

In the early days of Legal Island we bootstrapped everything. The company was started with a £500 loan from a family member. We kept overheads to a minimum by employing only homeworkers, who worked through the Internet. Salaries were met through income from the next event, and sometimes only just. Early employees could see how tight things were with the complete absence of any extravagance in either our business world or our personal lives. Moreover, we were throwing everything we had at the business to make it viable and successful.

When we announced to our employees they may have to wait for the bonus we had promised them until the cash flow improved, there was a distinct level of discontent. This surprised us. Surely they understood how difficult things were? Yes, they did, but what we later came to understand was that they didn't have the same emotional investment in the company as us. It was unfair to expect them to make sacrifices we were prepared to make for the business to work. Lesson learned, don't confuse your own commitment to your destiny with those of your staff and when introducing a profit share bonus be clear about the boundaries. Don't lead anyone up the wrong path – facts and clarity mean a lot.

Remunerating and competitive advantage

We believe that to gain competitive advantage you need to do two things well:

1. Remunerate in a way that minimises the cost of employment but maximises the benefits passed on to the employee;
2. Remunerate in a way that suits your type of business but also motivates staff – or at least doesn't demotivate.

We will look at both of these in this chapter and we'll call the first one 'mighty clever remuneration' because we like fancy, powerful titles.

Mighty Clever Remuneration

What's important to understand first of all is that salary is an extremely inefficient way of paying people. It's right to devote time and resources to making appointments on at least competitive salaries but not at the expense of working out how to pass on benefits to the employee most effectively. Benefits amplify employer money because, when done well, they cost less than the perceived value to employees. Clever SMEs move money from their payroll to the benefits account and get creative in terms of how to spend this money judiciously whilst providing maximum returns.

When we say this to fellow business leaders, they often reply that they head up a small business with just a few employees, and with no scale to bring in attractive deals that they can pass on to staff. But we think you can box clever here by offering scale by clubbing together with other SMEs. Offering to refer people in to other SMEs helps too. Those working in the benefits industry understand that the best way of getting into the large companies (and securing big paydays) is to catch them when they're small. So don't forget to share your plans for growth with them at an early stage.

Four top benefits attractive to employees are: health plans, health insurance, critical illness cover and pension contributions.

Health plans

In return for a small monthly payment per employee by the employer, staff can receive cash back up to maximum amounts on several health-related items. Our health plan covers optical, dental and certain therapy costs. Staff can also access medical advice online, get expert second opinions, private consultations and use certain scanning services (MRI, CT and PET scans). In addition, there is a 24-hour advice and information line included for counselling, legal, health and wellbeing advice.

Left to their own devices some employees will inevitably put off that trip to the dentist, doctor or optician due to time and money pressures. We give them the time (for every medical appointment an employee needs, they receive 2 hours paid time with no cap to the number of appointments) and money, so they have no obstacles when preventative healthcare is needed. Prevention is indeed, better than cure.

Health insurance

Employers can pass on value to employees by offering a separate private medical insurance policy for those situations where the NHS cannot offer a sufficiently prompt service. This not only gives peace of mind that serious conditions can be treated right away for the cost of a small excess (reclaimable under the health plan), but also that the many consequences of ill-health for the employee and employer can be minimised. Optionally, we also extend this to include partners and dependants, reimbursed through the payroll, which gives employees the benefit of corporate insurance rates that are much more competitive than individual family policies.

Critical illness cover

Employers providing this type of cover can do so far more cheaply than if employees were to take out the cover themselves. At Legal Island, if a critical illness is diagnosed, not only will speedy treatment be assured with the medical insurance, but employees have the comfort of knowing that a separate policy is in place that could pay them two years' salary to allow them to recuperate without added financial stress. Hopefully, they will never need this safety net, but it covers those serious long-term conditions that SSP or an occupational sickness scheme, run by a small employer, wouldn't be designed to cope with.

Pension contributions

Recently regulated, it is now compulsory for employers to pay some pension contribution on behalf of an employer, but voluntary contributions over and above the legal minimums can also prove attractive to employees and are not subject to tax to a certain limit.

Other Benefits

It is also important to remember that some benefits can be passed on to staff at little or no cost. They simply require research or a little imagination. These include:

Staff discounts (on your own products) – these are not taxed and can be an attractive benefit, whilst discount schemes for other products such as Perks can provide welcome discount on a range of items for staff willing to wave the card in the right places. We have one member of staff who has saved an estimated £500 using her discount card since we started the scheme three years ago.

Company loans to employees – these are not taxed (with a cap currently at £10,000) and may help employees to save a lot of money on interest for big ticket items, such as a new car, annual travel pass or school fees. Later we'll talk about conditions that should attach to such loans. One local business leader we know loaned a few thousand pounds to help an employee get out of debt that was spiralling out of control. It was a risky initiative, but she said it paid off in terms of the commitment and loyalty she gained in return.

Childcare vouchers – these can be provided tax free. Currently there's a limit of £55 per week for employees (with a lower limit for higher earners).

Cycles – there are several cycle to work schemes, such as cyclescheme.co.uk, that will allow employers to pass on benefits to employees to save 20%–40% on the cost of a new bike. And remember, if you're feeling really generous, bicycles provided by an employer are not liable to tax or National Insurance.

Car spaces – parking spaces at or near to work are tax free and are a welcome benefit for some employees.

Don't forget too that National Insurance is payable on most taxable benefits in kind.

Total Reward Statement

A few years ago, an employee came to us to say she was resigning. She explained it was simply a matter of pay as she had been offered more elsewhere. She gave us the proposed salary figure, perhaps hoping we'd ask her if she would like us to match it, but we didn't. Instead, we asked her if the salary also came with health insurance and the many other benefits we offered at the time. She said she didn't know but would check. The following day she withdrew her notice after she discovered that her prospective employer's benefits package was nothing like as good as ours.

The lesson for us was that we weren't communicating our offer to our staff well enough, if at all. To rectify this, we decided to issue all staff with a Total Reward Statement. This lays out all the benefits they receive as well as salary. In our first year we got it a bit wrong, because we detailed it right down to the milk we provided in the fridge for free. Jokes came back that loo paper would appear in the next statement. Lesson learned, be clear but careful about just how far you drill down.

A copy of our current Statement is included in the Appendices.

What About Pay Transparency?

New legislation in the UK came into force at the beginning of 2019 requiring some employers to disclose annually and explain, their bosses' pay and the gap between that and their average worker. Presently, it relates only to listed companies employing more than 250 employees and is a long way off from requiring full pay transparency in the workplace. But the trend appears to be towards greater pay transparency at work because this is seen by many as the best way to combat unequal pay between genders.

There's also a pragmatic reason to go for full transparency, which to us appears increasingly compelling. However hard you try to keep salaries confidential, for every employee who actually knows what others are on you'll find at least two others willing to sit down and idle away too much time trying to work it out. But full transparency is a tough challenge, especially for SMEs that have grown organically over time and may have many pay disparities that have accrued over this time. On one level this appears very unfair, but pay disparities develop because the labour market operates within the same laws of supply and demand as most other markets. When the labour supply is plentiful salaries remain more or less level. When it is not plentiful, employers have to appoint by offering salaries that include a premium, even when they represent a tough reach financially.

Of course, in good times the business leader could choose to increase existing salaries every time another equivalent employee is appointed on a better rate. But this is time-consuming and a difficult task which may upset pay parity issues in other parts of the business. It's also an exercise that is even more difficult to do in the opposite direction. Imagine asking staff to take a pay cut to align with new appointments made in a downturn. It's a non-starter, short of course of going in with the hatchet and explaining that it's pay cuts all round to stay afloat.

Early on in the development of Legal Island we had an employee who thought she had been paid incorrectly. She showed her monthly payslip to a colleague who had been there longer than she had and was in an identical post. It clearly revealed she was getting paid slightly more than her colleague. That colleague soon left.

This of course is just what primatologist Frans de Waal would say is likely to happen based on his experiment, where two monkeys trained to perform a simple task were rewarded with a piece of cucumber. Both were happy with their cucumber reward. After a while, one monkey was given a better reward (a grape) than the other for the same task. Immediately, the second monkey kicked up, throwing the cucumber away, suddenly very disgruntled. Lesson learned ... if even monkeys can rate fairness, treat humans differently at your peril.

We've yet to operate full pay transparency and we don't expect to get there soon. Some things are a work in progress. Leading a business is about assessing priorities, and pay transparency for us, at the moment at least, is not top of our list.

2. **Remunerate in a way that suits your type of business but also motivates staff – or at least doesn't demotivate**

So how do you remunerate staff in a manner that suits you and your business? Many SME leaders we know regularly state that they are more than happy to share the spoils of their success when times are good and set up reward systems to achieve this. But the best ones breathe with the company. They need to allow the SME to get back to payments that are more conservative when times aren't so good. Breathe out, pay out. Breathe in, keep in.

Our first attempt at devising a scheme to encourage team performance was crude but actually turned out to be quite effective. We informed our staff that we'd pay for a long company weekend away in Latvia at the end of the year after we heard that a budget airline had started a new route to Riga. The clever bit came when we told them about their accommodation. We explained that if they managed to sell 80% of places at our key events they'd be accommodated in a two-star hotel in the city. If they manged to sell 90% they'd earn a stay in a three-star hotel. Selling 95% would mean a four-star stay, and selling out completely would get them five-star luxury. One employee at the time immediately announced to everyone that she had never stayed in a two-star place and didn't intend to. We countered that we had better work together to save her from 'two stars and four cockroaches', and the game was on. (In fact, we had already provisionally reserved the three-star hotel just in case).

Each week the sales figures were posted on a specially constructed noticeboard so that the staff could follow their progress. Two weeks before we were due to fly we struck gold and sold the last event seat. We learned a lot from this first attempt to drop in a company incentive scheme. It had to be real, visual and within reach. We liked the message too: work hard and succeed and you'll be rewarded for it. Sometimes in the past we felt that some employees at least lost sight of the connection between success and profit and their remuneration.

Today, at Legal Island we have two company-level payment schemes over and above individual salaries. One is based on results relating to key events that we do. The other is based on our annual performance figures. We regularly review both of these because we know they have their faults. One fault is that underperformers reap the rewards of others who may be excelling in their roles. Another is that the schemes require a lot of rules to be drafted around them. For example, what happens if a member of staff leaves halfway through the year? What happens if someone is on leave (sick leave, maternity leave etc.)? What's the situation if we decide to cancel an event? The biggest drawback of the company performance scheme is that it can discourage us from thinking long term, preferring to give the staff good news of healthy profits and share-outs rather than reinvesting monies for future growth.

We're still arguing as to whether it's right to weight payments in accordance with salaries instead of a flat, equal share. Some think this is unfair whilst others think it's okay, because responsibilities are generally reflected in salary. This is why, currently, the event bonus is a flat share and the company performance bonus is weighted on salary.

ONE-OFF
THANK YOU PAYMENTS

When offering a general reward bonus, for example, at the end of the year, our experience is that it is best to offer a suite of choices from which employees can make their choice. You may think you're being generous by offering free weekend spa experiences but someone, for example, who is not body confident, may not thank you for a present requiring them to peel off their clothes, especially in an environment in which one or more of their colleagues may happen to be around. Bonuses of a similar value spread across leisure, shopping, household, entertainment or holidays work best in our experience.

SURPRISE, SURPRISE

One way we treat staff is through an exercise we call 'Surprise, Surprise'. This works as follows: from time to time we invite everyone to enter their names into a hat for random selection to win a surprise prize. The catch is that we tell them nothing about what the prize is, only where they will need to be and when, and how they will need to be dressed to benefit from it. The understanding is that whatever they win they must accept and do and it can't be transferred. To date, employees have won a trip to the ballet, a VIP night out at BBC's *Sports Personality of the Year Awards*, a foraging course and a one-hour drumming lesson with a musician from a well-known Queen tribute band. Of course, there's an element of reward here but it's also about encouraging staff to take a bit of risk and step out of their comfort zone, to do something they wouldn't normally do.

Individual Incentives – Beware the Bear Traps

Surely it makes sense to reward better those who produce the best results? After all, so much in the workplace is about fairness so why should the person who is showing little commitment and loyalty, and low productivity get the same bonuses as the top performers? In any event, how are you going to incentivise the top performers to stay and help the company perform to the next level?

Actually, we believe that on closer analysis it makes sense to reward only those employees in very specific roles, and then with great care. For tasks that are highly routinised, with standardised outputs, rewarding on measured performance may well make sense. Why not pay the person on the conveyor belt for every toy doll assembled or the fruit picker by weight of fruit picked? However, the truth is that with the development of modern technology and AI these jobs are rapidly decreasing in number. Sales are still the preserve of the incentivised payment but here too the research shows that such payments need to amount to relatively large sums to be at all effective. This is generally considered to be at least 10% of salary and preferably nearer 25%.[3]

Performance-related pay is difficult to implement too because the truth is that whilst results will be directed by the individual's efforts, they'll also be determined by how good the products and services are, how effective any surrounding marketing campaign turns out to be, how flush customers are feeling and how well the economy is doing. These are all factors upon which the individual has absolutely no control. So, our advice here is to think carefully and ask yourself whether you have posts inside your business that lend themselves to direct incentivisation by pay? If you do, then give careful consideration to how you're going to do it. Even if you do this you may prefer not to pay by linking it directly to performance. Instead you can monitor performance through good performance review work, regular feedback and by paying a competitive salary up front.

Outside of very rare exceptions we don't link pay to performance. This is for two reasons:

1. **Adequacy of performance measures** – to measure the performance of a full range of staff across many disciplines requires sophisticated performance

---

3   Law Donut https://www.lawdonut.co.uk/business/employment-law/pay-and-pensions/remuneration

measures that we do not have. How do you rate fairly the performance of an office manager, the office cleaner, the events manager, the operations manager, the PR and marketing officer, etc? To do it well requires a large time investment, which is a resource we believe is better spent elsewhere.

2. **Consistency across staff** – we're also concerned that different managers would assess performance differently. There's a risk here of damaging some working relationships, with some staff being rewarded and others not, determined in part by who they are managed by.

Remember what we said earlier: even monkeys get upset when they believe they have not been treated fairly.

Top HR Hack: In 2008, as we went into recession, we knew we had to act quickly because training budgets are the first to be slashed when times are hard and they were, and still are, our main source of revenue. Our payroll was by far our largest expense. In agreement with staff, we decided to cut hours rather than slash pay. Employees moved to a four-day week. The thinking was that at least this would give them a day to find work elsewhere if they needed to make up the shortfall. It also allowed the company to avoid compulsory redundancies. By the end of our financial year we had made a small profit, which we promptly passed on to our staff. We avoided going into the red by a lot of hard work from the staff. It seemed only right that they should benefit from any profits we made that year.

Benchmarking Salaries

Earlier in this chapter we touched on the importance of understanding market wage rates. This is best done by periodically conducting a wage or salary benchmarking exercise. This helps to improve retention rates, keeping at bay other employers from poaching your employees. It also proves to be an attractive recruitment tool that helps to showcase your organisation as one that is keen always to pay competitive salaries.

Recruitment companies are a good starting place for information on current salaries. Their websites feature latest salaries for particular posts compiled by reference to hundreds of employers. Websites from recruitment companies such as Hays, Hudson and Total Jobs are a useful starting place.

For our last benchmarking exercise we employed an outside consultancy company. We asked them to assess our current salaries against market rates at the time and to make recommendations for adjustments. We informed our staff that we were doing this exercise and that we planned to follow through on their recommendations whether or not we agreed with them. This proved challenging for both parties. There were some employees who were visibly upset when they were informed by their manager that they were assessed as performing a role that did not merit an increase. Others questioned the credibility of the consultancy firm (although interestingly only those that did not receive a pay increment). Equally it was hard for us to introduce increases for employees who we felt were already being fairly remunerated or even overpaid as it was. But the process was important because it introduced a large element of independence and it helped the staff to understand that any decisions were not based on their performance but the market rate for their particular post.

CHAPTER TWO

Wellbeing

The content of your character is your choice.
Day by day, what you choose, what you think
and what you do is who you become.
Heraclitus

Key Observations

- Being in employment is good for wellbeing but being in great employment is much better for all of us
- Workplace wellness is relevant to much more than attendance rates. It extends to productivity, creativity and positive human interactions
- Small businesses can punch well above their weight offering great wellbeing initiatives by teaming up with others and benefiting from scale
- Wellbeing is much more that Fruitbowl Fridays. It requires careful thought and a sustained approach

---

Introduction

Ever wondered how it came to be that in addition to all the other things a small business has to worry about there's the concern for the very mental and physical welfare of the people it employs?

The "I've enough on my plate movement" school of business leadership is frequently reminded that employees will spend up to a third of their 24 hour day and sometimes more at work. This is sufficient to require the person in charge of that time to have at least a moral duty to make sure that part of the day is not only not harmful to them but actually a positive experience. If a majority of people working in the private sector are employed by small businesses it should come as no surprise that employee engagement is prevalent in large employers but also making headway in smaller ones too.

A Short History of the Wellness Movement

In 1817, the great British social reformer Robert Owen first called for an 8-hour working day. He coined the phrase "eight hours labour, eight hours recreation, eight hours rest".[4]

One of the first organisations to implement Owen's ideal on a wide scale in the United States was the Ford Motor

---

4   The first group of workers to achieve the 8 hour day in the UK were the Beckton [East London] Gas Workers. Under the slogan of "shorten our hours to prolong our lives" a strike soon spread to other gas works. After some weeks the bosses capitulated and three shifts of 8 hours replaced two shifts of 12 hours. https://en.wikipedia.org/wiki/Beckton_Gas_Works

Company in 1914. After seeing the increase in Ford's productivity, and a significant increase in profit margin (from $30 million to $60 million in two years), most competitors eventually followed suit.

The modern worksite wellness movement began in the late 1960s and early 1970s as companies such as Boeing launched anti-smoking campaigns for their employers.

It is perhaps not surprising that wellness programmes first took hold in the US where employers are the main funders of medical care for staff and therefore eager to promote better health to keep insurance premiums low. The UK proved not too far behind with many employers offering staff by the 1990s and 2000s attractive health care programmes. With increasing concern about the standards of health care in the UK employers offering private health care benefits are proving increasingly attractive to work for.

Well-being Strategies

Today, the business case for corporate wellness services has been won. It's not about "if" any more, but "how".

It's accepted that wellness is not only about attendance rates each year. It is also be about the number of days that employees are too burnt out at work to be at all effective. Good wellbeing strategies help:

- reduce sickness absence;
- increase levels of creativity and innovation;
- improve decision making;
- boost staff working relationships.

26

Practical Considerations

Whilst the case for well-being in small businesses is strong the business owner needs to be careful to remember to observe the fine line between encouraging well-being activities in the workplace and insisting on them.

Directives requiring staff to exercise, eat only good food and when and how to spend their leisure time will quickly meet resistance and push back. They may make some feel genuinely uncomfortable and even cause a few to leave.

As many small business leaders are right in among their staff they can often see first hand what appears to them to be very obvious areas for improving employee health. It's very tempting to make judgments and comment accordingly.

In the very early days of Legal Island we had a staff member who seemed to drink nothing but coca cola all day long and spent many of her breaks outside puffing cigarettes. Her attendance record was poor with her often calling in to complain of chest and breathing difficulties. Every time she called it was hard not to offer her advice in terms of making simple life adjustments, but we manged not to. We knew if we did it would be a step over the line and a step too far.

The Four Components of Wellbeing

Good well-being is done over time and is more than just token fruit in a bowl on Fridays. It requires a sustained and well thought out strategy focusing on four areas. These are:

Physical health, Mental health, Workplace Environment and Financial Health.

The Employee Wellbeing Wheel

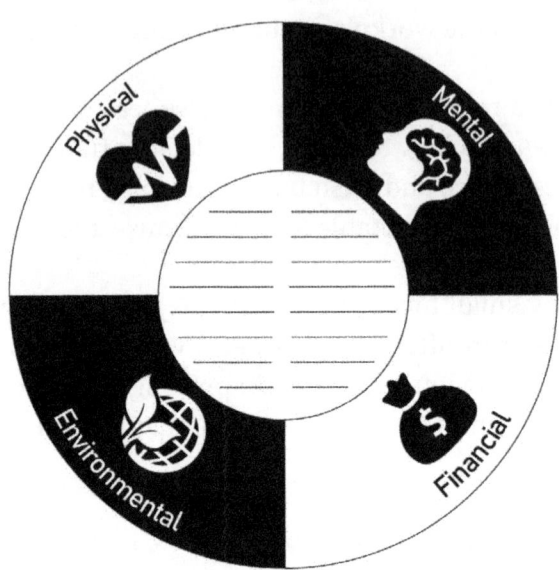

When we introduced the wheel into Legal Island we began the year by asking staff for their views on where they would like the company to focus. The plan was that as each item is introduced into the company or carried out it would be added to the wheel. Staff would immediately see the progress we are making and be constantly reminded of our commitment to their wellbeing in the workplace.

In the past we thought we had it sussed. We created a quarterly health and wellbeing worksheet and circulated it to staff – job done. But without the staff's buy in these worksheets were simply meaningless, albeit colourful, pieces of paper which either remained hidden in a folder in the employee's inbox or placed on their pinboards to tick a box.

Having realised how meaningless this activity was, we took the advice we apply to all engagement activities now and we enlisted Champions for the project with staff having a key part in the planning of the strategy. Effectively it becomes their choice of wellbeing initiatives.

Without a doubt Champions are key to the organisation and engagement. People in your team who get what you're out to achieve and want to take on the responsibility of seeing something come to fruition and be a success are one of your biggest assets.

Let's consider the four areas now.

Component One: Physical Activity

Physical inactivity is now identified as the fourth risk factor for global mortality[5] so it's not difficult to find government sources of assistance in this space. This most usually comes in the form of information on how to keep fit and active.

Small businesses often start by subsidising things such as gym membership and exercise classes. Today, such activities can be encouraged by a plethora of

---

5   Global Recommendations on Physical Activity for Health, Geneva: World Health Organization; 2010.

widgets and gadgets available relevant to the world of health and fitness. With Champions at the helm and staff buy in, these can become welcome perks for some employees.

It's truly amazing to consider what can be attached to some part of the human anatomy for a reading of some kind measuring steps taken, inner balance, heart intelligence, calories burnt, BMI and even the predicted date of your death! See deathclock.com if you dare.

Whilst many larger employers are beginning to replace the machine dispensers that drop down unhealthy snack options the small business can make their own contribution to healthy eating by ensuring that there is enough equipment at work for staff to prepare their own lunches.

Increasingly, employees prefer to bring in their own food knowing that lunches purchased from local shops are likely to be either from greasy buffet bars or highly processed or both.

Liquid intake is important too. At Legal Island we always make sure we have a good supply of non caffeinated drinks on hand. Water quality is also important. A while ago we sent samples of our office tap water away for professional analysis. The results showed that the water in the office was healthier than the bottles of water many staff were buying in. We saved them money and an awful lot of plastic.

Whilst we encourage a celebratory culture we are careful what we fund to supply this. We have a preference for independent food restaurants with imaginative menus over fast food outlets where the menu is standardised and the food highly processed. We ask external suppliers delivering lunches to provide plenty of sandwiches with granary bread and a healthy soup to accompany them. "If we fund it we call it" resonates with us. If we don't, staff are free to eat and drink what they like.

We've had a workplace nutritionist visit to do one-to-one reviews of staff eating and drinking habits over a given period of time. She then makes recommendations for change. For some such an intervention appears to have had little or no impact. For many, however, it's been life changing with them modifying their eating and drinking patterns to help them lose weight, have more energy, give up a bad habit or simply just eat more healthily.

We've also had guest speakers on new foods to try. We've had team building days in kitchens learning how to create new wonderful dishes. We've been on food tours too of our capital, Belfast.

Occasionally, we've availed of the (often free) services offered by the public and third sectors in the health space. One organisation did health checks with us privately advising some staff that they were close to being classified as overweight. This proved to be advice that jolted many in into action.

We've heard about a few organisations who have experimented with walking meetings. Instead of meetings around a table they hoof it around the park presumably with notepads and pens in front of them as they try not to fall into duck ponds or get soaked in the inevitable Northern Ireland rain. We like to get the most out of meetings making them as brief and effective as possible so this idea doesn't work for us.

Motion does however. We have some meetings standing up. In the longer meetings we might change places half way through just to help blood circulation and we try to encourage staff never to sit in the same place each time they go into a meeting just to shake things up a little bit.

Component Two: Mental Wellbeing

Today, well-being is as much about mental health as it is physical. Our understanding of wellbeing has certainly evolved since the 70s when the habit of smoking was first directly targeted by employers.

ACAS recommends a tri-partite approach to mental health in the workplace. This is where employers are visibly committed to positive mental health with managers who are informed and open to conversation with their supervisees about mental health. Finally, employees are self-aware and willing ready to ask for help when needed. For their part the employer must:

- lead and embed a well-being strategy;
- reduce stigma;
- tackle the causes of workplace stress;
- support and train managers;
- understand the impact personal issues can have on mental wellbeing.

As a base position it means providing a working environment in which staff can thrive in an atmosphere in which they feel their dignity is both protected and respected.

Mental well being will never exist where employees are bullied, harassed or otherwise emotionally abused. Ensuring this type of behaviour doesn't happen in your workplace is best done by having a dignity at work statement, which is properly embedded into the organisation and complemented by training on dignity at work issues. This may seem a daunting task but strip it down and the requirements do not appear too cumbersome. It has three components:

- A Dignity at Work Policy and there are many of these available online for free;
- Efforts to implement the policy. You need to ensure it is actively profiled in your business and cross referenced in other policies;
- Train staff regularly – this means at least every two years preferably annually. This may appear a big ask but don't forget with the popularisation of e-learning it can often be done quickly and on a tight budget;

SEVEN QUICK WINS TO BE HAD FOR MENTAL WELLBEING AT WORK

 ## 1. MENTAL HEALTH FIRST AID TRAINING

This started in Australia and is now firmly established both sides of the Atlantic. Mental Health First Aid is an 8-hour course that teaches you how to help someone who is developing a mental health problem or experiencing a mental health crisis. The training helps you identify, understand, and respond to signs of addictions and mental illnesses.

Go to **www.mentalhealthfirstaid.org/take-a-course/**

 ## 2. MINDFULNESS PRACTICE

For anyone who has never tried mindful practice or meditation (we don't trouble ourselves with labels) and doubts its usefulness we challenge you to try this very simple exercise. Try sitting down crossed legged with your back to a wall or sofa and concentrate on nothing except your breathing for just ten minutes. We predict you can do it for no more than ten seconds before your mind starts to wonder and drift off to think about something that happened yesterday, or you are planning to do tomorrow.

You see, your brain is a muscle and it needs training just like any other. Training to help the brain stay in the moment has many benefits. It helps with attention and focus. It helps employees to single task which, today, is considered to be one of the most powerful work techniques and valuable skills of all. But don't just take our word for it.

34

A leading leadership organisation, the Ashridge Institute, recently found that business leaders who performed mindfulness training of ten minutes a day over a period of 55 days performed better across a range of leadership skills than those who did not.[6]

Mindfulness is not difficult to do even if you don't have the time to attend classes. Apps such as Aura and Headspace take absolute beginners through daily guided courses at a cost that makes the funding of them by employers very manageable.

At Legal Island we've trained a number of business leaders in meditation techniques as well as many of our own staff.

3. ONLINE BEHAVIOUR

Encourage staff to regulate their use of social media and the Internet by discouraging business contact after core hours. Let them know it's okay to turn their phones off or onto airplane mode after 6p.m

4. THE IMPORTANCE OF SLEEP

One of the most important books published in recent years is "Why we Sleep – The New Science of Sleep and Dreams"[7] by

---

6   "The Mindful Leader: Developing resilience and collaboration through mindfulness practice" https://www.hult.edu/en/executive-education/insights/the-mindful-leader/

7   Why we Sleep – The New Science of Sleep and Dreams, Walker, Scribner, 2017

Matthew Walker. He argues that we have to break out of this cultural understanding that getting by on little sleep is something to be warn as a badge of honour. It's actually foolish and bad for our health particularly our mental wellbeing.

Many employers provide staff with information on the importance of good quality sleep, training courses and some even provide time for cat naps and the couches to do it on.

 ## 5. PROVIDE AN EAP (EMPLOYEE ASSISTANCE PROGRAMME)

This is ideal for staff who may be going through a difficult time at work or in their personal lives. A basic programme may simply provide access to a 24 hour help line while others might come with an entitlement to up to six counselling session free of charge. The cost of these are not as expensive as you might think. But their main appeal to business leaders is that when something is clearly challenging an employee there's a designated path in place for them to follow.

This features professional advice and assistance – something preferable to the business leader having to weigh in and offer direct support of their own.

6. MENTORING AND COACHING PROGRAMMES

These are a great way of providing support in an organisation that helps promote emotional stability and mental health to flourish. In the past Legal Island has cross coached or mentored with other small businesses offering our more experienced employees out as coaches to help more junior staff in other companies and vice versa.

It's important to remember that coaching and mentoring is a giving experience too. Those who deliver it often get as much out of the process as those who receive it. It really is win-win for everyone when it is carefully set up and works well.

7. GRATITUDE

Time and again research shows that people who practice gratitude tend to be happier than those who don't. But its "practice gratitude" that is key here. It's more than acknowledging what you are grateful for.

The easiest way to do this is to write thank you letters or notes to people. Some people do not like to be publicly thanked or praised so a handwritten letter or email can be much more welcome and appreciated.

Gratitude jars are sometimes used too where individuals drop in notes mentioning things they're grateful for which are read out from time to time. One of our employees took our jar home to pilot it with her family. She tells us it was a big hit with everyone especially at Christmas time when her family opened up all the notes inside as they reviewed the year.

Component Three: Environmental Wellbeing

An environment conducive to strong productivity would appear to be the cornerstone of every workplace but not every employer gets over this first hurdle. Too often staff are in cramped or confined workspaces that are poorly lit or ventilated. Noise levels from other staff members, incoming calls, computer servers or copying machines disrupt the silence.

Finding accommodation to suit current business needs and also future needs is probably one of the most difficult tasks for small businesses. Afterall, there is so much out with the control of even the best run businesses that predicting the office space you'll need in three years' time is an exercise fraught with danger.

When taking premises do you go for more space which you hope to grow into as you expand and hope you can absorb the costs? Or do you take just what you need accepting you'll have to start the time consuming process of finding new premises in two to three years? It's a tough call.

Whether the working space is limited or ample it can be easily improved by focusing on the following:

Air quality

- Keep your air vents open and unblocked and replace filters regularly. As a general rule, air filters should be replaced every 6-12 months;
- Maintain a healthy level of humidity. Humidity between 30 and 50 percent helps keep dust mites, mould and other allergens under control. Use dehumidifiers and air conditioners to control the humidity level in your office. You can buy hydrometers online to test humidity levels for as little as £30;
- Clean spills immediately. Excess moisture or residual dampness encourages the growth of mildew and mould, which has severe health risks;
- Don't forget the importance of fresh air. When weather permits, keep windows and doors open to maximise circulation of air.

Light

Intelligent use of light can really improve an office environment. We human beings need good quality light far more than we realise. It's important to note the following:

- Fitting LEDs will save money and provide a better quality of light. Fluorescent tubes have long been the bulb of choice for many offices. They're cheap to buy and fit and suitable for use in suspended ceilings lighting large areas. But flicker and buzz as they do it's not surprising they are being replace by LEDs;

- Use natural light where possible. The objective should be to make employees feel connected to the outside world whilst being able to work comfortably. Clever use of mirrors can increase amounts of light as well as the feeling of space. According to a recent study, workers operating in windowless environment had reduced energy levels and poorer sleep patterns compared to those with natural light;[8]

- Lighting suitable for every task. Experts remind us that a modern office demands its own type of lighting to suit the requirements of the people working there. With the popularisation of open plan offices many workspaces are becoming flooded with artificial light as ceiling lighting has to be strong enough to illuminate everyone's desk. The result is glare from overhead fluorescent lighting and over-illumination, which can have a negative impact on an employee's health.

Bring nature into the office

Plants are clearly an employee's best friend at work. They improve air quality, help reduce noise and improve office aesthetics. Some organisations now make use of what is known as a living wall or vertical garden while others might have a small garden outside where organic vegetables are grown for staff lunches.

---

8   Impact of Windows and Daylight Exposure on Overall Health and Sleep Quality of Office Workers: A Case-Control Pilot Study" 2014 https://www. ncbi.nlm.nih.gov/pmc/articles/PMC4031400/

Noise reduction

Noise is one of the most common complaints raised by employees working in corporate office settings. A study from the University of Sydney in 2013[9] found that lack of sound privacy was the biggest frustration for employees.

Reduction techniques in your office might include:

• Noise Friendly Flooring – carpet or vinyl is to be preferred over hard flooring surfaces like natural wood, porcelain and ceramic. These can wreak havoc within a work setting due to the massive amount of noise pollution they create.
• Dedicated Quiet Space – empty meeting rooms make for great makeshift work sanctuaries. Whilst some employers have a designated quiet spaces within their office layout;
• Noise-Cancelling Headphones – perhaps the best solution to noise for those on a tight budget is noise cancelling headphones. Good pairs can be sourced for as cheaply as £80 online with more expensive ones claiming 100% noise reduction. These use microphones and a special processing technique to create an opposite sound wave than the one headed for your eardrum.

But noise reduction is about people too. So why not try experimenting with a no Talk Tuesday where, for half a day at least, staff agree to have no unnecessary chat?

---

9   Workspace satisfaction: The privacy-communication trade-off in open-plan offices, Jungsoo Kim, Richard De Dear *Journal of Environmental Psychology* 36:18–26 · December 2013

Office ergonomics – join the get Britain standing campaign

An increasing amount of work is done around a screen sitting down. With fewer items faxed or posted nowadays even the reasons to get up from the desk seem to be dwindling. Any physiotherapist will tell you we're just not designed to be seated for such long periods of time which may be why lower back pain is the cause of so much absence in the workplace. So why not encourage staff to stand at their desks?

Before you predict a mini riot let us temper that last suggestion by advocating that employees are given the option to do it and can switch between standing and sitting throughout the day.

Quality sit/stand desk stations can be purchased online for around £200. Yes, we agree that's a sizeable expense if you have a workforce of ten all wanting to join the pilot. But £2,000 is a snip of the cost to your business if one of the ten is off for more than one month with a back related issue.

The anecdotal evidence too from one trial in our office is that working at a sit/stand desk is not only good for your back but it also improves thinking as the body moves and the mind stays sharper.

Of course, such a move should be accompanied by a workstation health and safety assessment which would check that the new arrangements support improved posture and a straighter back at the work station.

Component Four: Financial Wellbeing

Ok so you pay your staff every month and now you're expected to help them manage it too?! Before you complain that this job of business leadership just contains far too much in terms of expectation, allow us this paragraph to make the case as to why it's in your interests to do it. In fact, we can do it in one sentence. It's an area in which you can pass on considerable value to an employee at little cost to your time and your company budget.

It's generally accepted that personal financial education was always done badly at school if done at all. Yes, now schools understand its importance but there's so much pressure on the school curriculum that it is rarely afforded sufficient time. Financial education begins at work and with you.

Here are some quick wins to jump in with which should help staff engagement levels.

 Ask a finance expert to call in and offer tips on good finance management and investment. Many will do this for free in the hope of picking up new clients and leads .

 Start a fun virtual investment club in which staff members can gamble millions of virtual pounds whilst learning about how to invest. Winners get a voucher and the kudos of feeling mega rich.
See for an example **www.virtualtrader.co.uk**

Consider loaning amounts of money to staff at better than market rates. You may decide to tie this to longevity of service and with clauses that clearly set out what happens if the staff member decides to leave before all repayments are made.

Cash rich companies can score easy wins by offering to loan employees money at favourable rates that may help them out and ensure they don't descend into an amount of debt from which it may prove difficult to recover.

 Offer access to pension advice and a pension contribution over and above the statutory minimum that incentivises employees to save ahead and to stay in your organisation.

Finally, it's our experience that many small business leaders have a size complex. They take the view that financial benefits including visits from finance experts are likely to be offered only to organisations of a certain size. If you're of that view we'd encourage you to do two things. First, explain to those you are reaching out to any plans you have to grow. Early contact with you as a business that one day may employ hundreds of people might be worth the time investment. Secondly, consider joining up with other small businesses so you increase your buying power. They'll likely give you more time if you speak on behalf of your business and several others.

CHAPTER THREE

Values, Vision, Mission

*The bravest are surely those who have
the clearest vision of what is before
them, glory and danger alike, and yet
notwithstanding, go out to meet it.*
Thucydides

Key Observations

■ Line of sight is crucial for every employee to understand their own purpose in an organisation

■ Employees who understand the meaning of their job role and its wider purpose tend to work harder than those who don't

■ Be clear on your understanding of each term — "Values", "Vision" and "Mission" (VVM)

■ Understand that as your business evolves, your VVM will need to be revised

■ New opportunities should not be rejected because they don't fit your VVM but they should be kept firmly in mind every time new opportunities are considered

Introduction

There are two types of forests not far from our offices. The first, the mixed deciduous, possibly started by accident with trees growing in random patterns and places with paths that wind their way around them often in a clumsy and convoluted manner. The other is the coniferous. This is a carefully managed and purposely designed pine tree forest that presents the walker with corridors of trees perfectly spaced out that are easy to traverse. From the beginning of your journey of the coniferous forest you can already see the end or at least a place where you can rest and get your bearings.

Your role as the business leader or people manager is to have your organisation resembling the pine tree forest much more than it does the one that started with little or no planning.

Vision is all about designing your organisation's line of sight while your values capture the parameters in which you work to achieve that vision. Your mission explains how you expect to reach your destination.

Why is Vision and Mission so important?

A study in the US in 2007 [10] found that the results of telemarketers responsible for generating new university funds improved by a factor of five as soon as they were connected to a mission. Their performance skyrocketed

---

10   Impact and the Art of Motivation Maintenance: The Effects of Contact with Beneficiaries on Persistence Behavior, *Organizational Behavior and Human Decision* 103(1):53-67 · May 2007

when the university decided that the telemarketers should meet the students who benefited from their efforts.

The results were similar when lifeguards were informed about how many lives had been saved by vigilant lifeguarding. Lifeguards asked to read material that focused on personal benefits were not nearly as motivated – at least not in terms of their willingness to work extra hours.

In "Good to Great", Jim Collins notes that companies that focus on purpose outperform their competitors by a factor of six. First published in 2001, it is interesting to note that almost twenty years later, a survey of senior company executives indicated that only 38% of leaders believed their staff had a clear understanding of the organisation's purpose and commitment to its core values.[11]

Knowing that something needs to be done and done well is one thing; achieving it is something else altogether.

Practical Considerations

So how do we do Values, Vision, Mission well?

We need to start by understanding the difference between them.

Adopting company values can be straightforward enough.

---

11 McKinsey, Making work meaningful: A leader's guide https://www.mckinsey.com/business-functions/organization/our-insights/making-work-meaningful-a-leaders-guide

They often originate from the founders of the business and what they consider to be important when running an organisation.

At Legal Island, we highlight our core values on the steps leading from the ground floor to the mezzanine floor: Integrity, Quality, Responsiveness, Fresh Thinking, Passion, People Development, Business Relationships. We want everyone to be aware of these values – staff and visitors alike. Barry jokes he's always careful not to trip up on any of these steps – especially the one marked Integrity.

Integrity is huge for us. A while ago our Board met to consider how to achieve greater penetration into the Irish market. The subject of competitors came up and how to find out more about what they were doing. Someone put forward the idea that we could approach a key competitor claiming we wanted to buy them out and later withdraw having first gained useful insights into their business operations. Another board member immediately questioned the proposal against our declared value of Integrity and the suggestion was discussed no further. When we look back on this now we can see that it was undoubtedly the right decision. Had we followed through on the idea some employees would have known what we were trying to do and why. Rightly, they might have thought that if we could behave with such deception to competitors we might also behave with a similar lack of integrity towards staff as well. High levels of employee engagement are predicated on trust and we couldn't expect staff to trust us when conducting our business in such a manner.

A second declared value played in when a competitor approached us a few years ago to sell us a training product they had developed. It was demonstrated to us online and we had immediate concerns about the quality of the product. When we raised this with them they replied that most of their sales were generated at the end of the year where their customers (almost entirely lawyers) were desperate for CPD points and didn't really care too much about the quality of the training. We knew immediately there was little point in continuing the meeting.

VVM – Examples

The vision should outline what the business wants to be and it should have a firm focus on the future. A good vision statement should be inspiring and motivational:

"A world without Alzheimer's disease."
— Alzheimer's Association

"One day, all children in this nation will have the opportunity to attain an excellent education."
— Teach for America

"To be the most admired company in every market we operate in."
— Bassadone

A mission statement describes the objectives of the organisation and how it intends to achieve them. Its purpose is largely to inform.

The mission statement should answer the questions: What do we do? Why do we do it? How do we do it? And for Whom?

It's the roadmap for the organisation's vision statement. It is often drafted with customers, creditors, employees, competitors, investors, partners, shareholders and suppliers in mind. The following are a few examples of good mission statements:

"Build the best product, cause no unnecessary harm, use business to inspire and implement solutions to the environmental crisis."
– Patagonia

"Inspiring children and adults to find and express their unique voice through transformative, creative experiences."
– The Pushkin Trust

"To organise the world's information and make it universally accessible and useful."
– Google

The main difference between vision and mission is one of timeline. The former addresses the ultimate destiny of the organisation while the latter references what it is doing currently to get there. The two are often combined in a vision/mission statement. Our own is:

"To be the most valued provider of world class employment and compliance expertise and services, helping organisations get the very best from its people."

For business owners struggling with this, they might
want to ask themselves this question:

"In one hundred years, what do we want to be remembered for?"

This obituary approach to defining Vision and Mission can be very
powerful.

Both vision and mission statements have been much maligned in recent years. LinkedIn is full of critics quick to rubbish an organisation's vision and mission statement and indeed the need for either, pointing out that they are often nothing more than mere words rarely known by employees and that mean next to nothing to the consumer.

But the fact is, a good vision and mission statement forces business leaders to ask themselves what it is they want to achieve and what is the purpose of each core business activity. Business leaders should also explain this to their staff in short and simple terms.

Opportunities for Competitive Advantage

Promoting your VVM

If it's true that you need to hear something several times before it sticks, it's clear there is a lot of work to do the moment the VVM is signed off.

51

Employees conversant with their VVM generally work for organisations that regularly convey their VVM via a multitude of channels. They might use blogs, lunch and learns, posters, social media, staff days and quizzes to remind staff of key content. Many businesses reproduce their VVM on office walls as a statement of confidence in the clarity of their purpose and as a constant reminder of the value of their work.

As your business grows, you should regularly re-visit your VVM. Unless it's a period of exceptional growth, your VVM shouldn't really require updating more than every three years.

While line of sight is important, updating a VVM is a time-consuming process. It requires a lot of thought, planning and sometimes outside facilitators. It is wise to draw on the support of your staff when doing top end work – it's a clever engagement tool. But it's also a time stealer. Do not forget that for every hour your employees are looking at flipcharts trying to revise a mission statement, they are distracted from front line activity that's adding to the bottom line.

Employee Values

While many businesses have declared company values, only a few go far enough to draft employee values. We think this is a mistake. Adding employee values to VVM bookends the activity of an organisation nicely. It starts with the values of the organisation and it finishes with the values of its people. This is powerful.

Drafting and agreeing employee values is a process that should include employees from an early stage. In fact, at Legal Island, our employees were given free rein to draft and adopt a complete set of employee values.

A while ago, we asked our staff to come together, without any senior input, and devise their own employee values. A part-time junior member of our staff volunteered to facilitate the group with the mission of producing something they could all agree on. The result? A set of values they all agreed to, understood and believed in. They are now reproduced on both levels of our offices and reads as follows:

"Staff at Legal Island aspire to: Be respectful and tolerant, supportive and approachable, show integrity, trust and understand, consider their impact on others and practice what they preach."

These values are presented to anyone hoping to join our team – along with our "Here's the Deal" document. This outlines to the reader who we think we are and something about the culture of the company. A copy is in the Appendices. If potential employees don't understand the importance of these values, they are unlikely to be right for us. But they are also an important reference point for existing employees. Having a declared employee values remains the easiest way to point out to an employee when they may be deviating from the collectively-agreed minimum benchmark for appropriate behaviour – because they were the ones who adopted them.

At Legal Island, a former staff member was once heard to be very critical of another staff member in their absence. The line manager simply invited the staff member into a private discussion area and asked how that comment sat with the employee values that we have on the wall on every floor of our building. It proved far more effective than a threat or disciplinary warning, especially since the employee had been involved in composing the employee values. What the manager heard next was an immediate admission from the employee that they had overstepped the line.

Putting it All Together

At the beginning of our financial year, we try to put all key information into one place. We use "One Sheets" a lot. This is simply the requirement to condense lengthy documents into one place and onto one sheet. We've used them in the past to brief our Board, summarise key meetings and set out key people development objectives. They force the authors to get immediately to the main items of information and they save readers considerable time since they can quickly access key points.

We put the following information on a One Sheet at the beginning of our financial year which, in the past, we have laminated and handed over to staff as a point of reference. Many of them keep it near their desk on a wall:

- Vision/Mission Statement
- Strategy for the Year
- Key Themes for the Year
- Our Values
- Our Resources
- Our Quality Standards

Any themes for the trading year will be set out along with our values, a note on our resources and our quality standards. The section on resources reminds staff that although we are small, we have access to ample resources that, when used well, can make us highly effective. Posting our quality standards serves as a constant reminder of our dedication to high quality work.

A sample Strategy at a Glance page is given in the diagram below.

Strategy at a Glance

Our Strategy for 2020+
Growth: Greater efficiency. New products.
Continue to build and improve company structures and procedures.

Four Key Themes

Our Resources
Staff
8 Coaches/Consultants
First Class Office &
Training Facilities
Software
Huge Network of Contacts

Our Vision/Mission
To be the most valued provider
of world class employment
expertise and services, helping
organisations get the best from
their people...

We are Legal Island

Financial

Dashboards, event planning,
costs

Customer

Satisfaction rates, knowing
customer needs

Internal
Processes

Our Values
Integrity, Quality
Responsive, Fresh Thinking
Passion, People
Development,
Business Relationships

Our Quality Standards
Investors in People
(Platinum Level)
EFQM
5 out of 5

Mapping flows, Software
knowledge

Learning &
Growth

Develop individual & group L&D

CHAPTER FOUR

Job Design

*Choose a job you love and you'll never have
to work a day in your life*
Confucius

Key Observations

- Job design is overlooked as an HR discipline and is usually done very badly
- Job design is relevant to recruitment, optimising performance and retention as well as engagement
- Creative and innovative job design can produce considerable competitive advantage when done well
- The aim should be to create a culture where employees are responsible for outputs rather than tasks
- Methods of working have been completely left behind by developments in technology

---

Introduction

Understand from the get-go that bad job design can sabotage your chances of attaining real employee engagement.

In truth, many jobs are not really designed at all. They tend to be a mish mash of loosely connected tasks. They are often backed up by an employee handbook written in language which suggests that every employee activity needs to be regulated closely and restrained. To many, employee growth and development appears doomed from the start.

People who come to a task with little relevant training tend to be risk averse and work off default positions. That is why it is possible to see so many roles today with standard terms and conditions and the default working hours of 9a.m.-5p.m. But strip a job description right back and it's easy to discover that often the core purpose of the role could be done in a very different way and in a manner that would suit both the employer and employee far better. It's a commonly quoted story but one worthy of recounting here.

The guy who goes into the hardware store and says he needs a drill and a bit is actually mistaken. As the shopkeeper reminds him, he needs neither. He needs a five inch hole. A drill and a bit will give him this. But so will many other tools; some of which may be easier to source, cheaper and do the job more effectively.

Those concerned with job design need to ask themselves the right questions at the very start. These might include:

- Does the role need to be performed in the standard number of hours each week? (37-40 hours)
- Is it one post or could it be subdivided or carved into two or more posts remembering that part time workers bring additional benefits to a workforce?
- Do the hours need to be performed during the conventional 9-5p.m. window?
- Could the hours be done in part or in whole outside the standard place of work?
- Could this role be one that starts out as one with conventional design but morph into something different over time?

The aim must be to create a culture where employees are responsible for outputs rather than tasks.

Practical Considerations

When to do job design:

1. **When first drafting the job description and before recruitment begins.**

It's essential to think about job design well before you go looking for someone to fill the post. This is because you need to keep the recruitment pool as wide as possible.

Employers commonly make the mistake of thinking they'll negotiate more flexible terms only after seeing the whites of the applicants' eyes and feel confident that they can trust someone or at least begin the journey to trusting someone.

The pool will shrink considerably if you deter candidates from applying by posting a job description that appears fixed and gives no indication that it is really only a guide for parties to consider. Some applicants will be deterred from applying at all if they think that the first thing they'll have to do in an interview is negotiate new terms.

EXAMPLE

Advertise for a receptionist 9a.m.-5p.m. and you immediately risk disqualifying those who have to do the school run. Too bad. You need someone to cover the core hours of business, or do you? Work arounds might include diverting incoming calls before 10a.m. or after 4p.m. to a call centre, asking other staff to cover the phones during these hours (often quiet times in many offices) or letting calls run to an answer machine that provides a mobile number for urgent calls. An advert calling for a person willing to do between 27-37 hours each week at times to be agreed will considerably widen the recruitment pool. You'll thank yourself for giving the matter additional thought when you see the stream of people queuing up for interview and you realise that the only one able to do the fixed 9a.m.-5p.m. pattern of work was wholly unsuitable.

For a job design checklist go to Appendix 11.

---

2. When working with an employee after satisfactory completion of their probationary period.

As soon as you view a new employee as a permanent part of your team you should aim to have another conversation about flexibility around the job role. But don't forget at this early juncture he or she may still not have the courage or sense of job security to have an open conversation about what really matters to them in terms of job design. A really fruitful conversation here requires both patience and skill.

At this juncture it is convenient to draw on the work of Bob Kelleher a leading expert on employee engagement.

In his book on employee engagement, Bob Kelleher talks in detail about what he calls "Circular Reasoning"[12]. He states "what a person enjoys may not always entirely coincide with what they are good at doing." Likewise, what a person is good at doing does not always match what needs to be done in a business. He explains this with the help of the diagram opposite.

Exploring the Employee Engagement
'Three Circle' Principle

1. The first circle (1) asks you to consider what the individual team member enjoys doing. A truly engaged employee will enjoy what they do, and they will want

---

12   Employee Engagement for Dummies, Kelleher, Whiley, 2013, p53

Circular Reasoning
Employee engagement

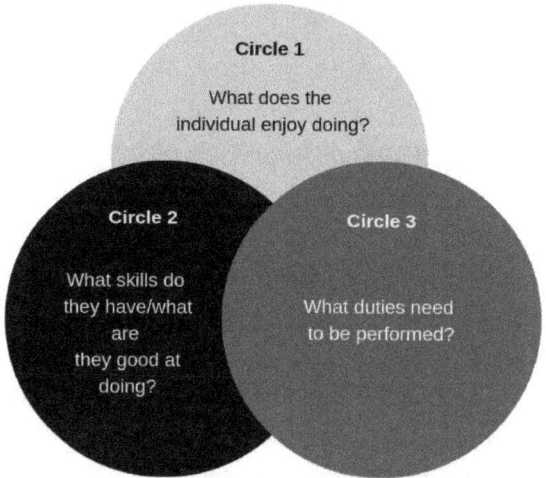

to learn more, do more, and grow in their role.

2. The second circle (2) asks you to consider the current skill set of the individual. An engaged employee has or seeks to obtain the skills to do the job well.

3. The third circle (3) asks you to consider the actual tasks that need to be carried out. Ultimately, we employ our people to deliver upon job-specific objectives and undertake a range of regular duties as part of their role.

Kelleher argues that the more significant the overlap between these circles, the greater the chances an employee will achieve full engagement. While it should be expected that what an individual is good at doing might not always coincide with what they enjoy doing, the ultimate goal is not to achieve perfect overlap. It is to take steps closer to that point, understanding the individual's needs, skills, and duties, in order to find a healthy balance between what works for them, and for the business. Good job design (or re-design) after successful completion of a probationary period its best done with the "Three Circle Principle" in mind.

Flexibility Around a Well Designed Job

At Legal Island flexibility is key and while this may not be a new approach, we cannot overstate how important it is to both the company and the employee. Sometimes it's not even something that is utilised but just knowing it is there should it be needed is reassuring. It helps the employee feel valued and unafraid to ask for a one-off change or something more long term.

Start time and finish times, as well as home working are flexible measures that can be discussed both at introductory level to the company and further into the job role for some employees. Compressed hours are common in Legal Island as are school term time shift pattern changes to help with childcare issues. Every staff member has an uncapped allowance of two hour medical appointments and leave can be taken in hours rather than set half days and full days. Time in lieu is in place and last minute leave is granted. Oh and we also give employees a day off on their birthday too!

Job Content

So you've a well designed job with built in flexibility. What's left? Oh yes content...! The shape of the job is important but so is the depth, the detail and the variety.

In the 1980s Hackman and Oldham developed what became known as the Job Characteristics Model[13]. This recognised five core motivational job characteristics:

1. **Skill variety** – the extent to which an employee is required to use a variety of different skills;
2. **Identity** – the extent to which a job involves the completion of a whole piece of work with end-to-end responsibility;
3. **Significance** – the amount of impact a job has and the contribution the job makes to the big picture;
4. **Autonomy** – the amount of discretion the employee has in making decisions about what to do and how to do it;
5. **Feedback** – the direct information given to the employee about the performance in the role.

In the very early days of Legal Island we had an admin team that was difficult to manage. They were poorly motivated. The quality of the work was unreliable and sometimes poor. When we look back now a major contributing factor was that we had given no thought to any of the factors above. If we had taken the time to explain how their role played a key part in overall customer satisfaction, mixed up their duties a bit and given them work that allowed them to see the journey of our customer into and out of the company we've no doubt they would have performed much better.

Even after forty years the work of Hackman and Oldman still merits careful attention, but the importance of the line manager's role has also been brought to the fore.

---

13   Work Redesign, Hackman & Oldham, Addison-Wesley, 1980, p81

Having a well-designed job will count for very little when overseen by a line manager who gives little or no meaningful feedback. We'll talk about the importance of strong communication in Chapter Seven.

Job Design and the Impact of Technology

Job design has certainly not kept pace with technology. Some (usually large) businesses have availed of the opportunity to contract out tasks either to other parts of their business empire or to other companies completely.

But many businesses still require employees to perform their tasks in the same place that they've always been done. "Your predecessors did their work from that seat and it worked. So you will too."

Today, not only could so much work be done more conveniently somewhere other than "the seat" but there are tools on the Internet for you to find someone to do it quicker and better by someone else too.

Websites such as Upwork and Freelancer are packed full of people with skills that could be harnessed for competitive advantage if an employee is encouraged to think creatively and be given enough autonomy backed up by a reasonable budget to contract out work that is not a natural fit with their skillsets.

Let's explain this point by way of providing a simple example. Example: Sandra is a marketing officer on a salary of £30,000 in a company of 20 employees. Sandra's boss has set aside a budget of £3,000 for Sandra to contract out work within the role that could be done better and quicker elsewhere. She is required to perform a variety of tasks. These include:

i   Annual budget reports
ii Creation of Powerpoint slides for business leaders in the company
iii Website and social media content
iv Harvesting email addresses and potential customer information from online sources
v   Content and design for their summer catalogue
vi Managing two marketing assistants

The first two items fall squarely within the range of Sandra's competencies. She's great with figures and is well trained on excel. Prepping power points slides is also a good outlet for her creative streak that she likes to make the most of.

Items iii-v, however, are time consuming and to do well require her to keep on top of so much that moves so fast. So, through the Internet she contracts these out to companies in the Far East leaving her more time to focus on what only she can do which is manage two staff that need bringing on.

Technology too provides us with the opportunity to reach out to people in a way that just twenty years ago we could never have imagined. Broader interactions enrich work experiences and provide with them opportunities for employees to develop new ideas, products and services developed by the access now available to people and resources.

Of course, with every advance there are disadvantages or

at least new issues that need to be closely watched.

Surveillance of employees is now much easier to do as GPS tracking, camera and software technology between them can account for where employees are and what they are doing at any point of the day. Whilst this brings many advantages it can cause considerable and unnecessary stress.

A study as early as 1989 by the National Institute of Occupational Safety and Health in the US[14]compared a group of heavily monitored clerical workers with a control group which was not monitored and found that the former group experienced a much greater degree of stress than the latter.

Technology too has also been responsible for reducing the expectation of turn around times. Until the 1980s and the popularisation of fax machines, many white collar workers at least had the leeway of 24 hours on a deadline. They could always claim an item of work was in the post when it had still to leave their desk. Now, if a piece of work isn't with a client or customer by a 12noon deadline an impatient sounding email or phone all can be expected just a few minutes later.

But it is also about our approach to technology and how we manage it that is important. At times we've all struggled with what might be termed "social needia" and the urge to be constantly in touch and communicating with others.

---

14   "Health Concerns – The Stress of Being Monitored is Killing Me" https://cs.stanford.edu/people/eroberts/courses/cs181/projects/1995-96/electronic-monitoring/health.html

The fear of missing out on news and what others are doing keeps many of us constantly logged in and flicking through Facebook, Twitter, and LinkedIn for far longer than we realise. It's not a good use of our time. It's not good for our mental health too. In his book "Digital Minimalism"[15] Cal Newport argues that we're just not "wired to be constantly wired" to the Internet. He points out that daily we need our down time and solace away from the influence of others. He recommends that we perform "lighting strikes" on the Internet. We get in, we find what we are looking for then get out fast and disconnect.

---

15   Digital Minimalism: Choosing a Focused Life in a Noisy World, Newport, Penguin Business, 2019

CHAPTER FIVE

Recognition

"People may take a job for more money, but they often leave it for more recognition"
Bob Nelson[16]

Key Observations

- Recognition done well is an extremely effective engagement tool. The good news is it needn't cost a penny either
- Intelligent use of good recognition mechanisms can quickly boost workplace morale and motivate employees
- Recognition is a need across all genders and culture – the art is in the delivery
- How do you notice good work in an organisation? It's a critical question

---

Time after time employee surveys reveal that recognition features as the most important motivating factor after pay

---

16   Bob Nelson PhD, 1,001 Ways to Engage Employees, Career Press, 2018

and wellbeing. But the truth is we're not great at doing it. In fact, we're much closer to lousy than we would all care to admit.

Fewer than one in three American workers, according to Gallup research, can strongly agree that they've received *any* praise from a supervisor in the last seven days, as measured by the Gallup Q12, a 12-item survey designed to measure employee engagement.[17] In the UK according to one recent survey, 54% of employees felt their boss could do more to appreciate them. Employees who report that they're not adequately recognised at work are three times more likely to say they'll quit in the following year.[18]

Before we discuss the skill of how to recognise good work, we need to talk about the importance of noticing it in the first place. There's little point having managers teed up to pass on well-timed and crafted praise if they're not positioned to notice performance to begin with.

Regular meetings with supervisees not only help to keep communication lines strong but they are also a good opportunity to understand the challenges an employee is facing in any one week and how they are responding to them.

As someone's manager you may think you can understand a person's role from the work that you give them to do. But often this is only a part of their overall output. They may

17   "In Praise of Your Employees", Robison, J https://www.gallup.com/workplace/236951/praise-praising-employees.aspx
18   "Employee Connection A missed Opportunity Between Employees and Bosses" https://www.rewardgateway.com/thank-you-infographic-inside-world-global-employee-recognition

be involved in other team projects of which you have little or no knowledge. They may be doing extra work to cover someone's absence. You may also be unaware that they are caught up in conflict with colleagues that is impacting on their time.

One-to-ones remain the best way of putting a window to the work the employee is really doing. It's important for managers to listen to other staff for feedback on an employee's performance and indeed encourage a staff culture in which individual performance is readily acknowledged and referenced and accounts and stories of strong performance or commitment are frequently shared, especially upwards.

Practical Considerations

People managers should remember, however, that recognition is a daily recital and requires constant work and attention. Adding it to a manager's fixed agenda is never a bad idea. For those who journal or keep a daily log of activities at work a section listing recent recognition work or even a daily reminder of the importance to recognise often pays dividends.

It is important to remember that we're not all the same at work. Human beings are complex creatures. We all like to be praised in different ways.

Our neural pathways are each unique and impossible for others to fathom fully. People managers can save themselves a lot of trouble by just asking their supervisees how they like to be praised.

Ask your employees three simple questions :

- How do you like to be praised?
- Is your preference to be praised in front of your peers or more privately in a one-to-one with your manager?
- Is either or both also ok?

Then the manager needs to ask what would their ideal be in terms of receiving a small reward. Is the preference for chocolate, wine, flowers, a book token, theatre tickets?

But make no mistake this process is not always straightforward. Sometimes modesty can get in the way. So, think about the environment in which you make the inquiry. Face-to face is not always best. A short survey delivered paper style or via surveymonkey similar to the one we use at Legal Island, called "What Matters to You" may work best. A copy of this is provided in the Appendices.

Recognition also needs to be real. If an employee feels they are simply being taken through a process or picks up on a manager's insincerity the relationship is likely to crash and you can expect to drop a "dis" in front of the engagement you had been obsessing about for so long.

Here are five things you need to try to do every time you recognise.

1. Provide **context** – for example "you were under a lot of pressure last week and you could have chosen to

delay working on this project but instead you chose to come in early to get it under way"

2. Be **specific** – "I saw you sit down 10a.m. yesterday and revise the report continuously until it was perfect"

3. Describe the **impact** "The report read well, was accurate and was really well received further enhancing our name and reputation in an area very important to us."

4. Reinforce their **identity** "You've really established yourself here as a key member of our team and with someone with a great reputation for consistently high quality work"

5. **Congratulate** "I want you to know how much we appreciate your going the extra for us this week and so well done and thank you."

Performance Reviews and Recognition – Beware the Bear Traps on the Beautiful Country Walk

No section on recognition would be complete without touching on the issue of performance reviews.

They are of course a perfect venue for the dispensing of recognition, but they are also occasions in which employees can exit such reviews feeling very demotivated. This is because they've been critiqued to pieces and often by a manager who is either poorly trained on performance review issues, or with little people management experience or sometimes both.

Often, supervisees are presented with accounts of questionable performance from such a long time ago that memories are unclear in terms of what exactly happened how and why. On occasion the employee may have no recollection at all of an example referred to in which case they are likely to feel that the process is unfair, lacks integrity or simply leaves them feeling puzzled and exasperated.

It's no wonder that conventional performance reviews are on death watch at the moment with many organisations choosing not to amend or update them but to abandon them altogether. See Chapter Seven for more on how we do performance reviews in our company.

This is not the place to talk about developments in reviewing performance but it should be noted that the conventional style performance reviews remain a danger point and an opportunity to take a well-recognised employee who is highly engaged many steps down very quickly.

 Most effective "performance reviews" commonly have two features:

- A process of ongoing feedback
- A focus on how to get the best performance from the employee in the future rather than do a post mortem on the past 6 months.

At Legal Island we no longer do performance reviews in the conventional understanding of the term.

Instead, we treat performance as an ongoing weekly task that is best done by having regular one-to-one meetings with meaningful feedback provided by strong open two way communication.

Annual training focuses on these key skills.

 In his book "Winning"[19], Clive Woodward talks about how prior to his arrival the England rugby squad only ever met to analyse games that they lost.

This, he accepted, was vital to do. Afterall, you have to learn from your failures and find out why things didn't go well. But the mistake the old squad was making was that they never met when they won to analyse why they had been victorious.

Woodward soon changed this and insisted they met after every winning match to analyse carefully what happened.

We've called this practice having a "Post-Victoriam" in other words a post successful event analysis to find out why something worked so well.

The aim is to do three things:

1. Identify the practices that caused the success in the hope that you know what behaviour to repeat in the future;
2. Identify what might even be improved on a subsequent occasion;
3. Recognise the efforts of those in the group that led to the success.

---

19   Winning, by Clive Woodward, Hodder & Stoughton, 2004

We believe this process is extremely powerful and very motivating.

Recently, at Legal Island we organised a Diversity Gala/ Awards evening. Our events manager, Emma, had to really fight for the event working very closely with outside contractors to get them to produce exceptional quality on the night. Emma was exhausted at the end of the evening. Everyone talked about what a great night it was. To her amusement she heard some guests declare that the night was so well organised it "seemed to move along all by itself". The following Monday we met for a "Post-Victoriam" and identified the following key success drivers:

- A lead in time of reasonable length to give us enough time to get key people on board (which ideally should be extended next time around);
- An early request to all staff to watch out for possible contributors on the night (this helped to get everyone's buy-in from the start);
- Belief in the ability of each team member to do what they had been clearly briefed to do;
- A contingency plan should suppliers let us down;
- Strong leadership from everyone in the team to hold it together and give off positive energy even where outside contractors were proving difficult to work with.

The post-victoriam helped Emma recognise the efforts of everybody in her team that night and gave the company an opportunity to work out how to do it even better next time around. It was a win-win all round.

Recognition thrives best in a celebratory culture. So, a positive way to follow on from a post-victoriam is to celebrate outside of the meeting environment. This might involve cakes in the kitchen or lunch on the employer. The old favourite of drinks after work may not always be the preferred choice of many organisations. They know that real gratitude is best expressed in company time rather than in an employee's. Moreover, if it's in company time and expense it's usually much easier to corral staff together. Insist that employees must attend a social event outside of working time and the idea is destined to run into the long grass or at least meet unnecessary resistance.

Top HR Hack – It can be difficult to organise a Christmas party that suits everyone. Some people just aren't party animals whilst others like to party long and hard. Here's how we do ours. We inform staff the party is in two segments. We expect them to be at the first; the second is entirely optional. The party begins in the afternoon in our office where we have food and drink and lots of silly party games. The second part starts in the evening at a central city location where employees decide whether they should head for a pub, a restaurant or a night club or attempt all three.

Celebratory Cultures

To introduce or improve on your own celebratory culture you may find the following helpful:

- **Link celebrations to meaningful milestones** – there's a lot of message in milestones. Many employers like to mark meaningful milestones by celebrating new employees, turnover or profit achievements,

new branding, new productivity targets rather than longevity or number of years with a valued client;

- **Establish a celebration budget** – you'll be amazed the power a separate budget can have in terms of kickstarting and driving a new initiative;

- **Don't forget to be inclusive when celebrating** – have food and drink that includes everyone. Those who don't drink or do caffeine, the vegetarians, the vegans and those who are gluten intolerant shouldn't be made to feel left out. It's a great opportunity to show you've given thought to everyone in the team. Suppliers are masters of menus for all and can advise you how best to be inclusive in terms of what you are wanting to achieve;

- **Go for an activity that's new to everyone** – if combining a celebration with a team bonding activity many employers like to choose an activity that suits everyone and where they can be sure few people will already have that skill or tried the activity before. Perhaps that's why ten pin bowling and clay pigeon shooting are still common and exercises based on TV programmes such as cooking lessons and break outs and escapes are proving increasingly popular.

Some employers like to link team building with corporate social responsibility work. You'll be surprised just how bonding it can be to paint a fence, build a stone wall or decorate the local charity shop together.

TOP BANANA

At Legal Island at the end of the year we order online specially printed "Top Banana" cards giving one to each member of staff. We ask them to send it to the one person who has inspired them the most in the previous 12 months. It may be a supplier, a customer, or even a shop assistant from the local SPAR – anyone who has given great service, gone the extra mile or simply stood out for a really positive reason. The choice is entirely theirs.

The exercise has the following benefits:

- It helps to profile the importance of recognition in our company. It's a talking point in the staff room for a long time;
- It helps staff to understand how good it is to recognise the work of others;
- It often generates really good feedback which has a positive effect on everyone.

CHAPTER SIX

Learning and Development

"Being ignorant is not so much a shame,
as being unwilling to learn."
Benjamin Franklin

Key Observations

- Learning and development represents a major opportunity for SMEs to gain a competitive advantage quickly
- Good training can be devised on a reasonable budget through the creative use of resources; particularly those online
- It's vital to realise that a learning and development strategy is not merely reserved for large employers. It's an important recruitment and retention tool often missed by many SMEs

---

We human beings are strange creatures when you think about it. We know what's good for us (or so we claim) but few of us seem able to follow through and apply this knowledge. A recent report conducted by the Small Business Federation[20] revealed that 91% of small businesses recognised the value of staff training and development, yet just 43% were actively investing in it.

There may be several explanations for this.

Some small business leaders may consider that they are operating in survival mode, especially in their early years. A preoccupation with meeting short-term goals is unlikely to lead to an environment in which the owner/manager is thinking more strategically with an eye on the long-term benefits of effective learning and development. SME leaders often fall into the trap of thinking that there are certain types of employee management activity that are the exclusive preserve of employers large and lucky enough to have at least one dedicated HR person. These include activity in the area of diversity and inclusion, corporate responsibility and yes, learning and development.

The fact is that many businesses, both large and small, are competing for labour in several sectors in the UK. Whilst labour supply is often cyclical, the indications are that in some sectors, labour shortages can be expected for a considerable time to come. In both the UK and the US, there is said to be a severe shortage of quality coders[21], whilst shortages in data and information management

---

20   FSB(March 2016), "Leading the Way: Boosting Leadership and Management in Small Firms", <https://www.fsb.org.uk/docs/default-source/fsb-org-uk/leading-the-way-boosting-leadership-and-management-in-small-firms.pdf?sfvrsn=0>

21   Building the Digital Platform: Insights From the 2016 Gartner CIO Agenda Report

are being reported in the UK, Ireland and other parts of Europe[22]

The situation looks particularly challenging for SMEs when you look at the competition there is for the limited talent available. The likes of Deloitte, Kainos and PricewaterhouseCoopers offer debt-free degree-level apprenticeships whilst the UK armed forces run periodic TV adverts boasting of the skills you can acquire with them, whilst enjoying great foreign adventures and getting paid.

Opportunities for Competitive Advantage

So, how do SMEs position themselves to compete against employers such as these?

Small-sized employers can offer a level of flexibility and intimacy that you can't find in even the best-run large companies. They have more informal structures that may attract some employees who might otherwise fear being swallowed up and lost in a corporate body. New starters will join with the head of the company already in sight.

SMEs might offer employees the chance to join a business in which there are accelerated job prospects and the opportunity to lead a business, or play a senior role in doing so, quickly. Many SMEs are led by two or more de facto partners, where one started the business and the other was found from within.

---

22 Cooper, Zach and Walker, Dale (17 September 2019), *Data Scientist Jobs: Where Does the Big Data Talent Gap Lie?* <https://www.itpro.co.uk/careers/28929/data-scientist-jobs-where-does-the-big-data-talent-gap-lie>

Employees might even benefit financially in the event that the business is floated publicly and they are shareholders. It is rumoured that Purple Bricks made some of its early management team millionaires in 2016 after it was floated on the Alternative Investment Market.

So, taking into account everything outlined above, your recruitment pitch might look something like this:

We are a small friendly employer (with a heart as big as our plans) offering the following to all who join us:

- *The opportunity to experience being part of a closely-knit, highly effective team;*
- *The opportunity to see the impact of your work quickly and share in the satisfaction that it brings to us all here;*
- *The opportunity to get involved in activities outside of your normal job description;*
- *Regular feedback on your performance and progress;*
- *A learning and development programme that is shaped around you, your needs and your aspirations;*
- *Competitive remuneration and the opportunity to benefit from generous leave entitlement including extended leave.*

It's important to set out the benefits of joining an SME. But it is also important to bear in mind that your biggest recruitment pool today is millennials – and your recruitment language should speak to them. Although the exact definition of a millennial is debated, they are generally referred to as those people born in the period between the 1980s and 2000. Today, they comprise around 50% of the workforce in both the US and the UK, with these figures projected to rise in both countries in the future.

So, what do millennials want to see evidence of when looking for a new post? According to the Deloitte Global Millennial Survey 2019[23], many millennials now say they are attracted to businesses that have a positive impact on society. So, early shouting about company vision and values is a must. But the majority still rate travel as the top of their priorities, so leading with information on holiday entitlement, including unpaid leave that can be taken or extended leave after a period of service, is advisable too.

Retention experts commonly advise that employers can best hold onto millennials by :

1. Keeping the work interesting. Millennials will soon look elsewhere if the work doesn't interest or motivate them;
2. Remunerating competively. It's important to remember that pay is a major factor for millennials especially for those no longer living with their parents. They face higher living costs than any other generation;
3. Providing regular feedback. Millennials are accustomed to instant information and they expect to know how they are progressing at work. Regular open communication is what they expect;
4. Allowing flexible working. It's important to remember that millennials particularly, value their own choices and prefer to be judged on results rather than the

---

23 Deloitte (2019), *The Deloitte Global Survey 2019*, <https://www2.
deloitte.com/global/en/pages/about-deloitte/articles/millennialsurvey.
html>

amount of time they spend in the office. Remember, work is increasingly about results – not where it's done

5. Training them. There's an expectation now from millennials that they will benefit from ongoing training in the workplace.

Delivering Effective Learning and Development

The three different types of learning and development commonly found across any type of business are:

1. Induction training;
2. Skills training (including communication skills training for all staff, especially managers);
3. Individual-based Learning and Development.

Induction Training

Too many SMEs still rely on the old mantra that the new employee will "need to hit the ground running". It's like the first badge of honour that they're expected to wear, and it's most likely not the last either. As Dick Grote once said, "Hitting the ground running is a farce. You know what happens if you do that? You fall on your face"[24].

The main purpose of induction training should be to integrate new employees into the business and help them

---

24 How to Be Good at Performance Appraisals : Simple, Effective, Done Right, Dick Grote, Harvard Business Review Press, 2011, p5

understand the systems and processes operating in the SME. This is the best way of ensuring that unnecessary and sometimes expensive errors are avoided.

Good induction training should also help new employees settle in quickly in their new working environment. It should give them a sense of belonging and help them integrate and socialise with existing staff.

Inductions should begin with an induction pack containing the following information:

- A copy of the job description;
- An up-to-date organisation chart showing the current roles and names of employees;
- An indication of where the employee manual can be accessed;
- Copies of any key material relevant to the business, such as brochures or video intros to the company;
- A staff contact list;
- A safety induction, including evacuation procedures;
- Security access, including locking-up procedures, alarms codes and rules relating to lone working;
- Information on essential training to be completed in the first week of employment. This should include training on data protection, equality and diversity issues, and healthy safety matters.

The first day of a good induction programme should normally include introductions to staff (depending on the size of the business) or some kind of event/exercise that will help the new employee get to know their colleagues quickly.

At Legal Island, during new starter inductions, we ask them to do what we call the "Ebay Challenge". This is where they are given £10 and just one hour to find something of value to sell on Ebay for maximum profit. After they've completed the exercise, they're invited to lunch at a local restaurant with their new team members. It's a great way for everyone to take an interest in the new employee, and it gives them all a talking point. It's a lot of fun too. We deliberately don't give too many rules to each person participating to see how they chose to interpret the exercise.

A copy of Legal Island's Induction Check Sheet is included in the Appendices together with our New Start Information Pack.

THE E-BAY CHALLENGE

Skills Training

This type of learning and development focuses entirely on the needs of the business.

The training often follows a Training Needs Analysis (now sometimes called a Learning Needs Analysis), which is commonly conducted by an external consultant. It has three main objectives:

1. Understanding the performance improvement that is needed;
2. Connecting that improvement to skills, competencies or capabilities;
3. Deciding what employees need to learn and how.

Frequently, those conducting the TNA will also include advice on how to measure the effectiveness – or otherwise – of the training in the form of Return on Investment (ROI). We have yet to meet an SME leader who admits to having enough time to follow through properly on ROI data, but the idea is right.

One of the biggest challenges with any learning and development programme is to ensure that it leads to a change in the employee's behaviour. The training, whether classroom led or online, will have little or no impact however engaging and enjoyable it may be, if it doesn't lead to the employee changing how they do something when they return to work. According to research conducted by Dr Philippa Lally[25], it takes 66 days to change a habit.

---

25 Gardner B, Lally P, Wardle J. Making health habitual: the psychology of 'habit-formation' and general practice. Br J Gen Pract 2012; DOI: https://doi.org/10.3399/bjgp12X659466.

Knowing how long it will take us to change a habit or a behaviour is one thing but understanding how to do it is entirely another. The self improvement movement is replete with books on how to change habits particularly early in the New Year as we all make goals and attempt to keep to them. Trying to identify common threads between the leading texts in this area is difficult but many appear to agree that to change a long binding habit (or behaviour) you need to do the following:

1. Focus in on the habit you want to change until such time as the new behaviour no longer requires conscious effort;
2. Reward yourself after each reasonable period of time you clock-up demonstrating the new habit or behaviour (the "carrot");
3. Don't forget about the "stick" you may need to help you maintain your self-discipline. This doesn't have to be particularly foreboding; just effective. It might include something as simple as logging the amount of time for which the new practice is being observed. Breaking a long run is a powerful motivator not to regress.

 Many SMEs over-focus on skills relevant to specific departments such as finance and marketing, and fail to cover off general skills for all – especially on communication skills training for their people managers. This is a mistake. Good, strong, communication skills from managers to supervisees is a prerequisite for competent performance management and development. It should be an annual L&D item in every SME.

Individual Learning and Development

Smart business leaders will try to align business objectives with those of individuals. This is an SME's opportunity to mark itself out and to stand out to job applicants. It's also a great retention tool.

A creative L&D programme can combine or marry training required for reasons of business with a development plan that is specifically designed for a particular employee. Part-funding an apprentice scheme, a part-time professional qualification or even an MBA does require a sizeable budget and a time sacrifice, but it should bring in new business contacts, new expertise and help retain the staff member for at least the duration of the course.

Many SME leaders might also be open to funding self-development courses. These might be of the one-day conference type delivered by the likes of Tony Robbins or Paul O'Mahony, or courses over a longer period that concentrate on certain key characteristics such as building resilience, personal effectiveness and mental wellbeing.

What about the cost argument?

Perhaps the reason that so many SMEs have still to embrace the idea of proper learning and development plans is because they do the wrong sums at the start to assess their value.

A training programme costing £3,000 for one particular staff member might appear prohibitive, even when spread over more than one year. But when set against the cost of finding and bedding-in a replacement for that employee if they were to leave (currently calculated at between £11,000 to £30,000), the training appears to make complete business sense.

Yes, there is often a time sacrifice, but this is frequently offset by the networking value of the course, and the contacts that might be made whilst doing the training. Carefully drafted wording in contracts of employment can ensure that the employee stays for a reasonable period after the course is completed; or returns all or part of the costs if they do not.

Learning and Development on a Budget

Contrary to popular belief, learning and development doesn't always need to be expensive. Here are four initiatives you can take to really keep on top of costs:

- **Free Online Training** – avail yourselves of the huge amount of training that is now online for free. If you're new to this area, you might start with Barbara Oakley's popular course, "Learning how to Learn". Although she talks about learning a language in the course, what she advises is also applicable to learning many other skills. Other sites such as Optimize.me offer access to hundreds of summaries of self-development books which can be easily shared;
- **Form Cluster Training Groups** – join other SMEs in your area to form clusters that can share the costs of training. They may be in different industries or

even the same. Sometimes, even competitors should consider banding together if it means they can source a key skill that would otherwise be beyond their reach. Several years ago, we asked a top marketing specialist to work with us, but he wanted top-line rates to do it. We met his costs by inviting other local companies to attend his sessions with us;

- **Sharing Training Opportunities**. If you have a trainer who can take a maximum of 15 people, but you have only 12 staff, why not offer the remaining places to companies in your cluster in the hope that you'll be offered opportunities in return? Again, we did this effectively with coaching training. Not only did it bring costs down, but it gave all participants the chance to coach someone outside of their internal circle;

- **Government Subsidised Training** – avail yourself of the many free or heavily subsidised training opportunities that come courtesy of the government – local or national. For a useful list of these, see online.[26]

 Stay and Exit Interviews represent an important communication opportunity. Often, business leaders conduct the latter but not the former. Asking why an employee has chosen to stay with you can be very informative. If the feedback is that it's because of the learning and developing environment, you know your strategy is working. If it's not mentioned, there's an opportunity for the learning and development programme to be highlighted and its key benefits emphasised. Incidentally, we advise that you conduct an exit interview only when an employee has left employment and is settled in another post.

26 https://www.gov.uk/career-skills-and-training

He or she is unlikely to give you the truthful feedback you're really looking for when they know that they are still dependent on you for a reference.

A Workplace Learning Culture

There are many who argue that employees learn most from other colleagues. Certainly, the workplace is a great learning pool and should be treated as such. Many top-performing SMEs demonstrate a learning culture in which learning and development is seen as a shared obligation, but also a joint and enjoyable initiative. So, how might SMEs ensure there's a good learning culture in their organisation? Why not learn from one of the most successful companies; for example, what do Google do for their staff that is readily transferable to very small organisations?

Four initiatives they practise in this space include:

1. Employees are encouraged to declare learning goals. These need to be specific; "Learning SEO" won't do. "To summarise a Coursera course on SEO" is much better;
2. Journaling – not only is journaling a great way of keeping on top of your thoughts at work, leading to greater clarity of thinking and better problem solving, it's a useful record of learning day-to-day and over time;[27].

---

27   Ferriss, Tim (2015), *What My Morning Journal Looks Like*, <https://tim.blog/2015/01/15/morning-pages/>

3. Share the Learning – many SMEs make it a condition of attending a course that they summarise the learning for others in the organisation. For those that may need it, this is an important reminder that courses are more than time out of the office and will require focus, effort and follow-up work. At Google, they have a UserLikeThursday event in which quarterly staff are given an opportunity to present their learning on a subject of interest to them;

4. Bookshelf of Learning – Google has a library for shared learning, so why shouldn't SMEs have at least a book-shelf on which books of general interest and self-development are left for others to pick up and read? Ours is in our kitchen/diner.

CHAPTER SEVEN

Comms Interpersonal and Internal

"The single biggest problem in communication is the illusion that it has taken place."
George Bernard Shaw

Key Observations

- Most day-to-day problems in small businesses are a result of employee communication deficits
- Employee Voice is key and merits constant attention
- Remember, there's one thing worse than not listening to staff: pretending to listen
- Great employee communication is best achieved by employers who manage a dashboard of communication channels

---

Introduction

My first ever car (Barry) was a mini cooper. It cost me £200, second hand. The first thing I did was to join the AA with the £20 I had left to my name in 1984. I got to know the AA breakdown people quite well, for they were often out to attend to me. I noted that they always followed the same procedure when they first approached my car. First, they'd check the electrics, then the fuel supply and finally, structural issues. When I asked one AA employee why they followed the same procedure every time, he explained that 80% of all breakdowns were a result of electrical problems, so it made sense to check the electrics first when attending to a vehicle. For us, the equivalent of car electrics in a small business is communication. If something has gone wrong and we want to get to the root cause, we look for communication glitches first.

In the early days of Legal Island, we noticed that we were dealing with the same issues repeatedly, week after week. They weren't serious but were nonetheless time consuming and an unwelcome distraction. They included meetings that had to be postponed because key staff were working at home that day, last-minute, expensive copies of notes for delegates that we weren't expecting, and training that didn't achieve its objectives.

We tackled the issues quickly but soon realised that we were engaged in what effectively amounted to little more than "business first aid". We were attending to symptoms rather than addressing the root cause of the problems.

Eventually, we realised that the common denominator between many of them was poor communication. The more time we spent improving communication, the less we spent on unnecessary day-to-day problem fixing.

Practical Considerations

Good communication flow in an organisation happens when three things are working well. They are:

1. The organisation is communicating well with employees – put simply, you might call this **communication down the organisation**
2. Employees are communicating well with the leaders of the organisation – again, in simple terms, **communication upwards**
3. Employee to employee communication is effective – **communication across the organisation**.

Let's examine each of these now.

1. Organisation-to-Employee Communication

Communicating an organisation's purpose and direction starts at the very top with your VVM (Value, Vision and Mission).

For the sake of simplicity, let's assume a brand-new company is created to produce a fancy new type of widget. The owners, a husband and wife team, excitedly hire fifty employees to get their business started.

Their first task is to explain their Values, then work on their Vision and Mission before finalising their first draft strategy document. In the very early days of a small business, its trading activities may well change quickly and substantially as it attempts to bed into the marketplace and find its niches. In such periods of rapid change and possibly growth, it may be necessary to revise the VVM often. But outside of this start-up phase, it's an exercise that needs to be revisited no more than every three years. Indeed, more frequent work in this space may convince employees that the business owners are unable to prioritise tasks effectively.

This brand-new widget company would do well to adopt what is sometimes known as a "waterfall communications strategy". Communication cascades from the top (the CEO, the MD), to managers and employees. An organisation that communicates well top-down, will have made it clear to all key personnel that they are communication ambassadors who are responsible for conveying the organisation's message clearly and in a positive manner.

 **Top HR Hack: Embedding Strong Communication**

- Communication ambassadors should be both trained and evaluated on communicating the organisation's message.

It's a key skill. Blockages caused by leaders who forget the importance of conveying critical information, or worse, convey it in a negative manner, cause huge damage.

- Communication "packs" might be worthwhile, particularly in larger organisations. These might include a long-form interview with the head of the small business, providing an explanation of the organisation's goals for the year. They might feature written Q&As or FAQs that could accompany communiqués to cover off anticipated queries. It's hard to overcommunicate in such an important area.

- Communication channels – generally it is better to have a multitude of communication channels rather than just one. If an organisation has a workforce with a very definite bias (for example gender or age), it's advisable to choose at least one channel that will reach these employees effectively. For example, millennials might respond better to a short video clip setting out the organisation's goals for the year. Meanwhile, Generation X (those born between the mid-60s and early 80s) might prefer a fact sheet with key bullet points.

Whilst it may seem obvious to state that communication starts with VVM and strategy, it's perhaps surprising to note that it's at this early stage that it goes wrong for a lot of employers. A survey in 2001 revealed that a mere 7% of employees reported that they fully understood their company's business strategies and what was expected of them to achieve the organisation's goals.[28]

---

28 The Strategy-Focused Organization" by Robert S. Kaplan and David P. Norton. Harvard Business Review Press, 2000

Of course, in addition to conveying information relevant to the business's strategy, the top-down structure will also need to include communication which is relevant to day-to-day operations.

What is in the organisation's communication toolbox to help them do this, depends very much on the numbers of employees it has and whether they are located in one place or across several. The following is a list of the most common:

1. Annual staff meetings
2. Main section meetings – devised with reference to departments or locations
3. Announcement-led communication in the form of communiqués issued by email, or posted on intranets or on social media channel outlets designed for employers, such as Slack or Ryver.
4. Use of conventional mediums such as noticeboard messages and newsletters, as well as external media campaigns and the use of press, radio and T.V.
5. One-on-one meetings with managers/one-to-one meetings with others. The practice of meeting another employee of a very different level of seniority for coffee or lunch can really help with communication issues. One organisation we're aware of has a CEO who places a lunch card in the pigeonhole of a different employee every month, inviting them to lunch. He says, "I want to find out about their work and how it feels to them. But I also want to try to understand their journey with us and how we can both benefit from it."
6. Team and department meetings – done well, these are great mechanisms for communication. Even before

they start, employees can often share information that has relevance to organisational performance.

2. Employee-to-Organisation Communication

Of course, engagement is a two-way process and top-down communication is going to work most effectively if it is accompanied by strong bottom-up communication. Bottom-up is critical because it will give an employer an early indication of how well a new strategy is being received. This is often the first indication of whether engagement levels are likely to go up or down – or remain constant. But bottom-up is important for many other reasons. These include:

- New product and process ideas – employees are a good source of new ideas for additional products and services. They are also the first people who should be consulted when looking for better efficiency by introducing process improvements;
- Resource issues – determining resource allocation is a difficult exercise and one which is prone to a considerable amount of error. Strong bottom-up channels provide senior teams with early indications of whether a particular part of the business has been properly resourced;
- Employee disenchantment – when employees become disenchanted, action needs to be taken quickly. Office or organisational morale in a small business can be quickly dented by an employee who is constantly negative and continually finding fault. Strong bottom-

up communication is the best way for employees to vent and for senior leaders to respond quickly with fixes where they feel this is appropriate.

There's a great people skill in determining when a disgruntled employee requires immediate attention – and when the manager should focus energies elsewhere. Leaders have to determine whether the employee is simply in a dark place at work because of a personal issue which is causing them to gripe, or whether it is something more related to the workplace that is unlikely to disappear the next day.

We refer to it as the problem of the two "Is". Ignore, or intervene? This is a skill requiring a good deal of judgement and timing, but sometimes a bit of luck too.

Employee values (which we discussed earlier) may prove important here. Negative chat and gossip can be very destructive and such behaviour should be reviewed alongside the declared Employee Values. Many employers emphasise that such negative behaviour can be treated as a disciplinary matter, particularly where it amounts to bullying or harassment.

Hearing Ain't the Same as Listening

"Employee voice," as it is sometimes referred to, is a critical element of employee engagement. But securing good channels for upward communication is just the first stage.

The next is to convince employees that the organisation is actually listening. It is sometimes said that there is nothing worse than not listening to staff. We don't agree.

Pretending to listen is far worse. It smacks of insincerity and will quickly lead to considerable levels of disillusionment the moment employees realise they're in little more than a window dressing process.

So, remember, setting up good channels is essential, but that's only the start of the important work. Follow-through is critical and this means responding to communication in a prompt and meaningful way.

Good bottom-up communication needs to happen through multiple channels. This is because it needs to convey ideas for fresh products, processes and services, but it must also convey what the employee feels about their place in the company, how they are managed, how they relate to colleagues, their views on strategy and the organisation's values (and the extent to which they are being upheld).

It's important to bear in mind that the communication you require from employees covers the full range, from business suggestions to matters bordering on the personal.

It's advisable therefore to present to employees with a reasonable number of channels through which this communication can be made. An employee might be prepared to make a business suggestion via a suggestion box process because of the anonymity that allows. However, he or she might choose not to volunteer the same idea in a group process for fear of it being judged as unwise or misguided. Equally, employees might not offer feedback on a working relationship in a survey process because it creates a permanent record of what is said, but they may be inclined to share their views in a face-to-face environment with a trusted listener.

As a general rule, therefore, the more channels you can lay in front of employees to encourage the flow of information you need, the better. Good "Contact Us" pages on websites now carry as many communication channels as possible for a reason. Businesses know that the more channels they have, the more likely they are to hear from customers. Give them a variety of channels to work with and you significantly increase the chances of getting useful, thorough feedback. In the employer's toolbox here, you might find:

- "Stop Start Continue Change" Mechanism – this is where employees are invited to give their views on whether something in the organisation should Stop, Start, Continue or Change. When done well, it's a powerful communication tool, and one we use effectively at Legal Island. To use it at its best, it's important to set expectations and manage them carefully. See the Appendices for further information;
- Ideas box – in physical or virtual format; for example, a dedicated inbox;
- 360 Appraisals – conducted internally or by external consultants;
- Annual or bi-annual surveys of staff; for example, in the form of a Surveymonkey;
- One-to-one interviews which are often conducted by external consultants, such as those done when an organisation is heading for IIP assessment.

Communication and Safety to Speak

It is important to remember that there are many reasons why communication may not flow well directly upwards.

In small businesses, safety to speak issues are a definite factor.

For example, if a company is owned by two people who are also leading it, feedback relevant to their performance may not be forthcoming, however easy-going and approachable they may be. Good feedback which is well-meant but badly taken could jeopardise not only strong working relationships, but promotion prospects and even job security.

Employees are most likely to offer useful feedback when presented with a suite of channels to use, particularly if one offers a degree of anonymity or at least a process in which well-meant feedback can be carefully crafted and presented.

Surveymonkey can offer the former, while 360 Appraisals offer the latter – and sometimes both. At least one channel should be available to detect broken relationships between managers and their supervisees.

If it is true that good employees don't leave organisations; they leave poor managers, strong communication channels provide employers with the best opportunity to address a problem that is a constant cause of high turnover rates.

At Legal Island, we present our staff with a dashboard of communication channels. We do this because we hope staff will find the exercise empowering. We're giving them the opportunity to comment on existing communication channels in the company. They can feed back on whether they think there are enough, and whether existing ones need to be changed. Ideas for new channels are welcomed.

For ease of use, we divide the dashboard into three parts: one-to-one communication, small group communication and all-staff communication. Our most recent one looks like this:

"Legal Island Communications Dashboard"		
Individual	**Group**	**All Staff**
Weekly 1-2 -1s with managers	Weekly Team Meetings	All Staff Monday Meetings
Annual Staff Survey	Ad hoc Team Meetings	All Staff Team Building Days
Stay Interviews	360 Appraisals	Strategy Development Days
Exit Interviews	Team Building Days	Formal External Assessors
Stop Start Continue Exercise	Lunch Meetings	

DITCH THE
OPEN-DOOR POLICY

One of the greatest modern scourges of good communication in the office is the adoption of what is commonly referred to as "open-door policies".

These are probably the single most damaging idea to your organisation's communication strategy.

Why?

They give business leaders and managers an immediate get-out-of-jail card when confronted with a negative development which has been caused (in whole or in part) by a communication blockage.

They can then say, "Well, if they were unhappy, they could have told me. My door was always open for them to come in and talk to me".

Communicating well in an organisation is a lot more complex than simply leaving a door open. It requires careful thought and plenty of analysis.

We felt so strongly about this that one of us decided to give a TEDX talk on it. Google "Barry Phillips TEDX Open Door Policies" to access it.

Here are five immediate reasons why an employee may not step through that open door to communicate with even the most approachable of business leaders:

1. They don't feel they have the skills to relay the feedback in the way it needs to be;
2. There's a cultural issue. Some people may be from a culture that feels uncomfortable giving direct feedback;
3. They are new into the organisation and not yet feeling confident about working relationships;
4. There's an imbalance in terms of status and working experience between the two people either side of the door;
5. The process is too brave. Cross the threshold and there's no turning back. Feedback in a survey allows the employee to think again and revise it many times before sending it on.

3. Employee-to-Employee –
Communication Across the Organisation

In Nancy Kline's seminal work "Time to Think,"[29] she argues that strong employee communication really starts by organisations creating a Thinking Environment®. This, she writes, is where employees are given space to think, which in turn facilitates quality communication and interaction between staff.

The ten components of a Thinking Environment® are: attention, incisive questions, equality, appreciation, ease, encouragement, feelings, information, place and diversity.

Showing respect for others in meetings is an acquired skill. It means you shouldn't talk over others, rubbish their ideas, or engage in personal attacks.

But business leaders should play their part too.

A well-conducted meeting in which everyone has an opportunity to make a meaningful contribution requires skill. Good meetings don't happen by accident. They're often found in small businesses with meeting leaders or facilitators who have been well trained.

For example, a meeting designed to elicit new production ideas will go very differently according to how it is structured. Consider these two styles:

---

29   'Time To Think - Listening to Ignite the Human Mind' by Nancy Kline, Cassell Illustrated, 1999

- Meeting leader Type I announces that the purpose of the meeting is to find new process improvements. As the first process is suggested, two others wade in to point out why it won't work. No one else says anything
- Meeting leader Type II asks everyone if they understand the purpose of the meeting and whether any clarification is necessary. She asks everyone to try to come up with at least one process improvement idea, which she lists on a flip chart without comment. Everyone is asked to indicate which are their preferred top three. Each of these are then scrutinised by the group in the final quarter of the meeting.

Some business leaders feel it is acceptable to shout, raise their tone of voice, or otherwise make it clear from their body language that they're unhappy with a particular outcome, but the truth is that this type of communication rarely improves a situation; in fact, it often makes it worse. Communication within an environment of agreed employee values that apply irrespective of status is most effective. Nowadays, in schools, the teacher that shouts and bawls at pupils is generally considered to have lost control – and with it, all hope of educating children that day.

Bosses who are shouters might make for entertaining TV programmes, but the reality is that few actually succeed as business leaders surrounded by staff enthusiastically supporting them.

Communication and Conflict

Of course, communication can occasionally break down completely. This most often happens when relationships deteriorate to the point that only the most basic pieces of information are exchanged.

Resolving conflict in the workplace is time consuming, energy draining and sometimes quite expensive. A common method of resolving a major conflict is to invoke a grievance procedure. This enables one or more parties to call out an employee's behaviour or something they have done.

However, employers should encourage employees to use mediation in preference to grievance procedures to resolve conflict where possible. In our experience, grievance procedures can be very damaging. They can be destructive and divisive and seldom lead to satisfactory outcomes. Often, where one employee is deemed to have lost the grievance, they leave. On occasion, so does the "winner," as they feel the need for a fresh start somewhere else, away from the trail of issues that have been unearthed and of which many other colleagues may not be aware.

Employers should first attempt to resolve such disputes informally through the careful use of managers. Where this fails, and neither party is likely to face a disciplinary process, parties should be encouraged to use a mediation process. In the Appendices, you'll find a template Resolution Procedure we use for our staff. You'll see that staff are encouraged to resolve disputes informally first, then by mediation. The grievance procedure is there for staff, but is very much treated as a last resort for many types of cases.

Managing Performance Through Communication

Unless done well, the two words "performance review" can fill both employee and manager with dread every 6 and 12 months. Instead of being perceived, as many may wish, as an encouraging and positive experience, they are more often than not associated with stress and a certain amount of apprehension, neither of which are likely to help engage your workforce.

Traditionally, a performance review is a formal meeting in which managers evaluate an employee's work performance, highlight strengths and weaknesses, offer feedback and set goals. However, they can be time consuming, involve considerable paperwork and are often done badly.

A survey of 1,500 workers carried out by Adobe in 2017[30]showed the following results:

- 52 per cent were taken aback by the feedback they were given;
- 37 per cent left the performance review feeling resentment for their manager;
- 22 per cent of workers cried after the session.

---

30 https://news.adobe.com/press-release/corporate/performance-review-peril-adobe-study-shows-office-workers-waste-time-and

A poorly tackled performance review therefore is not just detrimental to the employee, but to the organisation as a whole. It becomes a process that no one wants to engage in and, subsequently, from which no one benefits.

What is good to see, therefore, is that more forward-thinking organisations have been moving towards a more relaxed and informal process, where performance reviews occur in the shape of casual, but crucially, frequent one-to-one check-ins and catch-ups.

When done right, these catch-ups can help employees understand on a regular basis what they are doing well, where and how they can improve, how their work aligns with company strategy and, often, how behaviour can be equally as important as performance. We have touched on the importance of employee behaviours in chapter three (Values, Vision, Mission, Employee Values) and it is important to reiterate here that behaviour should be viewed with as much importance as anything else when it comes to assessing an employee's performance.

The need for a change to how performance reviews are held, stems from the change we are witnessing in the workforce. We've already noted that by 2020, it is estimated that millennials will make up 50% of the workforce. For millennials, prompt and regular feedback on their performance is critical. Safe to say then, that the old, traditional format of performance reviews is not going to cut it for them.

The key to these conversations is the early intervention and opportunity they provide; correcting issues before they become insurmountable, recognising success and providing praise immediately, all of which help to prevent the surprises that can crop up in traditional performance review meetings in which everything is stored up to talk about at that one meeting, resulting in one or both parties being caught off guard. These regular meetings – and the emphasis here is on *regular* – mean communication can be vastly improved, a coaching approach is employed and alongside encouraging growth and development, employee engagement is fostered.

In the early days of Legal Island, we fell into the trap of conventional performance reviews and paperwork, following a very regimented structure:

- Weekly one-to-ones;
- Monthly one-to-ones to review performance ("mini reviews");
- Six monthly performance reviews;
- End-of-year performance reviews.

In a similar way to that which we describe above, we found that too much was being "saved up" by both employees and managers for the mini reviews and 6-monthly meetings. Not enough issues were being addressed when they first occurred. So, after a facilitated session led by an outside trainer, in which all staff were involved, we decided to make the performance review process a lot more fluid.

With consent on both sides and an understanding of how the process would work, we did away with the traditional style performance review and began the journey down the more casual route of weekly one-to-one feedback sessions with coaching at the core. Nothing was to be left stored up, and feedback wasn't to be given at a later date.

This new, improved process is constructed around a series of touchpoints which use a five-question meeting approach, providing a greater emphasis on coaching-style conversations and reflection on company and employee values as part of the discussion.

This process has proven itself to work well, because it encourages open and honest two-way feedback around performance.

Let's look at the process we follow along with the guide we like to call the "Listening People Manager" to assist managers.

To have a process like this work, it is essential that the managers are trained in the appropriate conversations. We found coaching models worked well for this and as such, we rolled out a coaching programme for all our managers to complete.

Now let's look at the process we agreed with managers and staff. You'll see it is simple, straightforward and easy to follow.

Process

The People Process

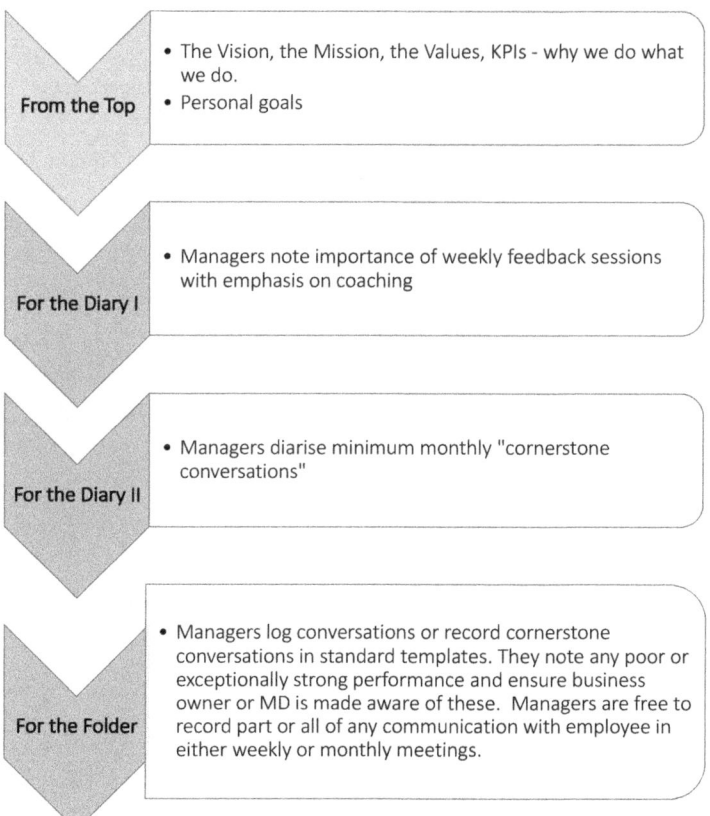

From the Top
- The Vision, the Mission, the Values, KPIs - why we do what we do.
- Personal goals

For the Diary I
- Managers note importance of weekly feedback sessions with emphasis on coaching

For the Diary II
- Managers diarise minimum monthly "cornerstone conversations"

For the Folder
- Managers log conversations or record cornerstone conversations in standard templates. They note any poor or exceptionally strong performance and ensure business owner or MD is made aware of these. Managers are free to record part or all of any communication with employee in either weekly or monthly meetings.

Next, we drafted a reminder to managers to help them implement strong communication with staff. In chart form it is represented as follows:

"Listening People Manager"

The Listening People Manager

Daily

- Ask your supervisee: "How are you and how are things going?" Remember this is not just a process you're going through. Employees need to feel you are genuinely interested in them and their work.

Regularly

(Every week)

- Ask yourself: "Have I touched base with my supervisee for feedback and to deliver support?" Did you remember to maintain a coaching style?

Regularly

(Min: every month)

- Ask yourself: "Have I met my supervisee at least once this month to have any one or more of the five cornerstone conversations?" If not, have you at least asked your supervisee recently: "Would you like to have a meeting about the five cornerstone conversations?"

Finally, we remind managers of the "Five Cornerstone Conversations" we encourage them to have with their supervisees regularly and at least monthly. If they don't

116

happen monthly, then the supervisee should at least be asked whether he or she would like such a conversation on a regular basis. We call them "Cornerstone Conversations" because, as we've said earlier, we believe strong communication is the cornerstone of every well functioning SME as well as being a key part of the supervisor/supervisee relationship.

"The Five Cornerstone Conversations"

The Five Cornerstone Conversations

Cornerstone 1: Learning & Development	• Ask: "Is any training accompanying the post adequate to do the role well and are there any parts of it still to be mastered? What may help you master these?
Cornerstone 2: Performance Objectives	• Ask: "What has gone well recently? Why is this and how can you get from good to great in certain areas? In there anywhere in which you feel you can make improvements?" Finally, don't be afraid to ask: would you like me to suggest areas for improvement?
Cornerstone 3: Work Processes	• Ask: "Are there any work processes that need to be improved and what would you need from me to support you in this?"
Cornerstone 4: Behaviour	• Ask: "How you would rate your own attitude, skill and knowledge when it comes to job performance ?" (its best here to ask for a 1-5 rating). Ask: "How may I be able to help you?"
Cornerstone 5: Job Satisfaction	• Ask: "How would you rate team and/or office morale?". Finish by asking: "How they would rate current job satisfaction?" (again, best to use a 1-5 rating here).

Our own experience has shown us that feedback from these conversations and a move away from old style performance reviews, has been overwhelmingly positive. Engaging in this type of process provides the employer/ manager with the opportunity to be less directive in their approach to problem solving, and a culture of coaching, accountability and greater use of initiative should ensue.

Should you decide to embark on a similar style of model, managers will soon discover that they no longer need the prompts or the question reminders; the style of the conversation becomes so natural that it forms part of their everyday communication. And good communication, as we know, is at the core of any good organisation.

There wasn't any particular model/framework/approach we were aiming for when we set out to revise our performance review process; we just knew that the way we were working was not working for anyone. It undoubtedly helped that we brought all staff along with us in the process, and having an outside facilitator was paramount to this. In the past, we had introduced new processes without early engagement, much to our detriment. This way, the staff were part of the building of the new process and owned it.

To date, we haven't had any issues with the new approach; one-to-ones are an invaluable way of keeping things on track. While this can take time, as long as everyone is brought on board with the process as it is implemented, they work for both the employee and the manager.

Top HR Hack Story: The Power of Listening. Finally, for the business leaders or trainers who would like a true story to share in order to convey the importance of listening, here's one from Barry's father-in-law who is Russian, and has a dacha (holiday home) not far from Moscow. He shared the story with Barry when they went to a nearby forest to look for mushrooms.

"One day, in the summer of last year, an elderly lady and neighbour of ours left her dacha in the early morning to go foraging in this forest. By late evening, she had not returned and a search party consisting of local volunteers was gathered to find her. By the end of the third day, there was no sign of her and the search was called off. Meanwhile, her son, who lives in another part of Russia, after three days of travelling, had finally made it back home. He asked the leader of the volunteer group what it was they had done to try to find his mother. He was informed that the ten volunteers had walked into the forest and had been asked to spread out as far as they could, whilst remaining in sight of each other. They were then told to make as much noise as they could as they walked forward in the hope that the old lady would hear them. The son thanked them for their efforts and then rallied a group of his own volunteers to go into the forest at the beginning of day four. He also asked them to spread out as far as they could whilst remaining in sight of one another. Crucially, however, he asked them to keep quiet as they walked forward. After a few hours, one of the party heard the cries of the lady who had fallen down a ditch and broken her leg. They managed to get a stretcher to her and take her to hospital, where she eventually recovered.

So, you see, listening is important. It can even save a life..."

CHAPTER EIGHT

Leadership

"What you leave behind is not what is engraved in stone monuments but what is woven into the lives of others"

Pericles

Key Observations

- Leadership for the top level of engagement requires skilful work with staff to get early buy-in and feedback on new business initiatives – but in this process, you should never forget that it is you who calls the shots
- Strong leaders work off a constant learning and development plan. They have time for their own development, simply because they choose to make time
- Despite what we see on popular TV shows, leadership is now by consent. It is no longer command and control
- Measuring engagement is an essential practice for any business leader

Leadership is changing.

The old command and control style is no longer evident in most organisations. Instead, you'll find people practising (or at least attempting) what is commonly referred to as "leadership by consent".

Undoubtedly, the advent of social media and websites such as Glassdoor has forced a level of accountability onto organisational leaders that simply didn't exist just a decade ago. We still have celebrity leaders on TV shows that turn the offensive treatment of employees into entertainment, but it's important to remember these people are neither role models nor typical.

In today's modern workplace, leaders who choose to shout and scream risk being outed and humiliating themselves. The organisations that employ this type of leader don't come out well either.

In SMEs, there is another consideration: there's nowhere to hide. As a business leader, you can't appear once a year to address staff and then return to strategising with your flipcharts in the seclusion of your office. Your staff will see you interact, they'll hear you wheel and deal, and they'll see first-hand how you respond to the highs and lows of being in business. They'll watch you closely when they know you've got bad news coming.

Today's employees don't expect you to be the leader who knows exactly what to do in any given scenario. They accept you're a human being, operating in a complex business environment. You are allowed to make mistakes;

but you're also expected to be humble enough to admit them and own them. Ouch! That's a tough ask sometimes.

You might say that today's leadership style lends itself to good engagement. The old-style leaders could bark and insist all they liked but they'd never get meaningful levels of engagement. New style leaders understand that early contact with staff on any given business initiative is advisable for many reasons. It secures early buy-in, it aids strong communication, and it helps to shape plans better at an early stage, when it's not too late or expensive to introduce quick changes.

But there's a trap for the unwary here. The aim is to seek views, not consensus. End up with the latter and you have something quite different: decision by committee. The adage, "A camel is a horse designed by a committee," should be a salutary warning. Business leadership is full of blunders that occurred because a decision was made by groupthink, by people who were not qualified to make it, in a process that was wholly unsuited for that level of decision-making. So, when thinking about employee engagement, let's not confuse leadership by consent with leadership by committee. The two are very different. The first is very desirable. The second is unwise and likely to be very damaging.

Leadership/Engagement Example One

A while back, we had just moved premises and were designing new letter heads, when the subject of naming our new offices came up. We got a group of employees together to brainstorm a new name. Our favourite before we went into the process was "House of Fives". This was because our aim is to get an average of five out of five on feedback forms from delegates, each time we run an event. We thought "House of Fives" would sit well with this and make for an interesting talking point, thereby being so much more creative than going for the obvious "Island House".

However, the group decided "Island House" was the best name. When we said we preferred to go with our own idea, one employee objected, "What's the point in getting groups together if you don't go with what we all think is best?" He had a point, but he was missing one too.

The French have an expression, *"L'esprit de l'escalier"* – (literally "staircase wit") which they use for the predicament of only thinking of the perfect reply when it's too late. What we should have said is that we had already decided on a name, but wanted to see whether there was a better idea out there. With their help, we had decided that there was not.

A friend of ours who heads a large quasi-governmental organisation in Belfast, has a great line to finish these types of meetings when he needs it:

"Well, there seems to be disagreement amongst us, but I'm employed here as the head to make the decisions. This will upset a few people and for that I'm sorry, but my decision is..."

Venture capitalist and management expert, Ben Horowitz, argues there are three high-level decision making styles :

1. My way or the highway – effectively a decision-making process that requires no discussion at all;

2. Everyone has a say – where colleagues have an input and the leader would call for votes if there was enough time. This can be a protracted process but everyone has a say;

3. Everyone has input, but then I decide. Here the leader seeks to maximise access to relevant information and brain power whilst keeping the process efficient by making a decision quickly.[31]

Horowitz argues the third style is to be preferred suggesting that style 2 drives everyone "completely nuts". He adds:

---

31   "What You Do is Who You Are – How to Create Your Business Culture", Horowitz,Ben 2019, p.223

"CEOs are judged on the efficiency of their process...and everyone has input then I decide tends to balance informed decision making with speed. It also acknowledges that not everyone in the organization has enough information to make a given decision, so someone has to be in charge of becoming knowledgeable and then deciding how to proceed".[32]

Leadership/Engagement Example Two

Shortly after we met to discuss the new name, we wanted to implement another change that required more than just views from staff; it required their active participation. It was a rule that no staff should eat lunch at their desks. We thought this would represent an improvement at work for two reasons. First, aesthetics. Lunches taken at desks inevitably leaves mess, which wasn't presenting well to visitors. Clients might arrive and see coffee cups and half eaten sandwiches at workstations. We've always worked hard to keep our premises and office looking smart. We do this not only because we believe it is relevant to good employee wellbeing (see Chapter Two), but it's about message too. If potential clients (and, for that matter, employees) arrive to see a messy working environment, they're unlikely to believe we're an organisation that is capable of producing outstanding results every time we do something. If you hop on a plane and find the drop-down tray in front of you is dirty, you may begin to question whether the airline can keep two engines running in the air for an hour when it's incapable of mastering the most menial of tasks.

---

32   Ibid,p224

The other reason we wanted to introduce the rule was that we noticed some staff weren't taking a break from their screens, which presented very real health and safety concerns. A few staff members would catch up on TV or play video games over lunch. By 5pm, their eyes were watering and their heads appeared fried. Our terms and conditions of employment clearly sets out an entitlement to breaks that is above the minimum required by Working Time legislation, but we had never gone as far as forcing staff to take breaks – nor did we really want to.

Before we acted, we conducted a quick Plus Delta analysis. Strictly speaking, this is a process most commonly used to analyse past performance, but we use it to help us assess options when considering a new business idea or an internal operational decision. It's more than a pros and cons chart, because we list anything that doesn't belong under the Plus heading, under the Delta section; for example, the opportunity cost of deciding to go ahead in terms of resource and time allocation.

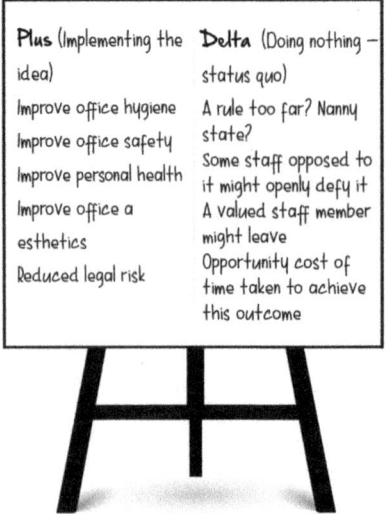

Plus (Implementing the idea)	Delta (Doing nothing – status quo)
Improve office hygiene	A rule too far? Nanny state?
Improve office safety	Some staff opposed to it might openly defy it
Improve personal health	A valued staff member might leave
Improve office a esthetics	Opportunity cost of time taken to achieve this outcome
Reduced legal risk	

This time, we outlined to staff what we were planning to do and our reasons for it. We sent them a survey asking for their views on the new rule, and what form it should take. Results showed that a few were neutral about it, a few thought it was a positive move and a further few were either against or even hostile to it.

First of all, we talked to the person who was strongly opposed to it. She stated quite forcefully that she felt it was tantamount to telling her what she could and couldn't do in her free time.

She added that there was nothing wrong with the present situation declaring "If it ain't broke, don't fix it". For a long time, this has been one of our most disliked sayings. Colin Powell calls it a "call to non-arms"; a charter to do nothing and never move forward. It wasn't a great start.

But we moved forward and introduced the rule for a trial four-week period, which soon morphed into an accepted rule and practice. One interesting benefit of the rule that we hadn't expected, was that it helped staff to circulate. There were more of us in the kitchen diner over lunch and better working relationships were formed as a result.

One of the biggest challenges for business leaders is determining whether to move forward with an idea or not. Sometimes, an idea may crash and burn because you didn't get enough staff buy-in from the outset, but no business leader can expect complete consensus before deciding to move forward. Brunel didn't build great ships, bridges and railway lines by first seeking consensus from those whom he needed to help him complete them. Helena Rubinstein didn't form one of the world-leading cosmetic companies by first seeking a consensus that it was going to lead to commercial success, whilst we'd also guess that Tim Schmidt spoke to very few people when deciding whether to create magical projects such as the Lost Gardens of Helligan and the Eden Project. Yes, of course, what your employees think about a given initiative is important. But it's not the only factor you have to consider before making your next move as a business leader. How you make good decisions and indeed, how you review them with a view to making better ones next time, is a complex question which is beyond the scope of this book. In fact, that's our second book. Stay tuned...

Incidentally, Tim Schmidt helped us in a way he's completely unaware of, and it goes like this...

Leadership/Engagement Example Three

About the same time we introduced the "No lunch at your desk" rule, we adopted another rule – or perhaps it is better described as a convention or understanding: we never drive into the same parking bay twice in a row. The idea here is that the first thing we do every day is something different to the day before. It led to the suggestion that we should try to avoid sitting in meetings in the same place, and to experiment with standing or moving around during long ones. We hoped it would help remind us of the importance of keeping things fresh and shaken up. This convention now features on one of our office walls, along with other things we strive to be, like the sound of and like to be reminded of. Just a year or two earlier, we

had tried to introduce much the same behaviours in our staff, but we were met with some resistance. What was different this time?

The answer was process and timing. This time around, it had been adopted by the group following a talk we had heard by Tim Schmidt. His wacky, enthusiastic style when talking about employee engagement proved infectious. That same day, staff met to ask what we could do to stir things up a bit and challenge ourselves. This time we facilitated – but they adopted. The difference was slight but also huge.

Working on Your Own Leadership Style

So many times, we've heard SME leaders state that they understand the importance of leadership training, but they just don't have the time to do it. But we know this is not true, and it's not because we have any familiarity with what they do. The truth is we all have enough time, but the lie we tell ourselves and others is that we don't. We use these comforting phrases to ease our way through busy, difficult business days. We all do it. But we need to be cautious, because these phrases can guide us away from action we should be taking. What we're really saying is, "We're not prepared to prioritise this at the moment".

 Next time you hear yourself say, "I don't have time," try this instead: "I'm not prepared to prioritise this at the moment". You'll be amazed at the difference this will make to your thinking and the impact it will have on your decision-making.

So, why should you prioritise leadership training? The answer is because there's a lot of research that points to the connection between strong leadership and good business performance.

Successful business leaders know that money invested in upskilling leaders is rarely money wasted.

If we've convinced you of the need to engage in training, where should you start? The good news is that today, accessing the type of learning and development that suits you best has never been easier. As well as the conventional half-day seminars and full-day conferences, there is e-learning, high level mentoring and coaching sessions offered by the likes of Vistage and Elite Online Training, not to mention an online Master's in Leadership, which is offered by numerous universities. Because training is so much more portable than ever before, it's easy to fit it into short bursts.

Let's look at some examples. Barry often listens to podcasts whilst cycling on his way to and from work. He rates Tim Ferriss, Rob Moore and Seth Godin as essential listening for leadership development. Jayne listens to audiobooks whilst driving to work with a preference for books by the likes of Michelle Obama, Oprah Winfrey and Arianna Huffington. Incidentally, she refuses to listen to anything on her way home. The return 30-minute journey is reserved for her to "normalise" her mind and get into family mode the moment she steps in the door.

Jayne has a particular reading interest in how to overcome obstacles in the workplace. This has a lot to do with resilience but also the flexibility and imagination you take to each challenge facing you.

 Try to exercise your creative muscle every day by noting down different ways to resolve a particular challenge you have been confronted with. It doesn't matter how small the challenge is, or indeed how realistic the solution is. It's the exercise of the mind and the act of stretching it that is important here. It can be business or family-related.

Example: the lawn needs cutting at home before it rains this weekend. Solution 1. Do it yourself. 2. Pay the neighbour's daughter £10 to do it for you. 3. Purchase a robomower to do it when you're not there. 4. Borrow a goat. 5. Replace the grass with astro turf so you'll never have to confront this problem again.

Measuring Your Own Effectiveness

The best way to assess your effectiveness as a leader who is aiming to secure high levels of engagement from employees, is to measure it. If you are responsible for engagement in an SME and you are not its leader, be sure to persuade the leader of the importance of this activity. Every SME must have a person who accounts for levels of engagement. It's hard to receive low scores and negative comments, but we take the view that it is always better to know.

There are many standard surveys you can use for this purpose, but the majority of them are designed for large employers. However, SurveyMonkey offer a free one on their website whilst Tinypulse.com offer good advice on how to design your own.

One important factor to remember is that whilst you may wish to improve the survey and adapt it as your workforce changes, it is best to keep some questions the same if you want to measure changing levels of engagement over time.

Before issuing the survey, it is advisable to set out what it is you are expecting of employees, and the purpose of it. For example, you should always indicate whether the process is intended to be anonymous, and the parameters of the feedback. You should also indicate what will happen in the event that someone discloses a comment that requires you to act; for example, they complain they are being bullied or harassed.

Before we conclude this chapter on leadership we want to mention our ten leadership principles. These we aspire to live by every day. We keep them printed out by our desk as a constant reminder that leading with employee engagement in mind is a tough role, which requires a lot of courage.

Ten Leadership Principles

1. You understand that opposition can be loyal and dissenters an asset
2. You fully support all initiatives and evade none
3. You support colleagues by sharing generously your knowledge and information
4. You are open to changing your mind even where to do so may make two decisions appear inconsistent or contradictory
5. You understand the quality of a person's advice does not always align with their status or experience
6. You make sufficient time to keep focused on the big picture
7. You never say you don't have time because you do. Instead, you acknowledge it's about how you prioritise your time

8. You aim to start now and get perfect later understanding there is no perfect time and no perfect working environment
9. You are careful to ensure there is no major disconnect between how you portray yourself to outsiders and how you are with your own employees
10. You understand that strong leadership requires moral courage and fortitude

The Coronavirus, Remote Working and Employee Engagement

The outbreak of the Coronavirus (COVID-19) in December 2019 forced many employers to consider homeworking for staff for the first time, at least as a temporary measure. For some businesses, this experiment with remote working helped them to understand the benefits of giving employees the option to work at home at least for part of the working week. They realised too that workarounds to obstacles presented by not having all staff in the office all of the time could be found with relative ease and with minor cost implications.

The essential components for strong employee engagement set out in this book apply to home workers just as they do to those who are office based. In many cases these components have particular relevance to the home worker. Points stressed earlier in this book about the importance of good job design, wellbeing and recognition are amplified when applied to homeworkers.

They're not in the office and in front of managers as often as their office based counterparts. There's less room for error before a disaffected homeworker resigns and goes elsewhere. Those who operate largely outside of the circles of influence within a business can quickly feel left out as well as left behind. A good manager is one who is alert to this and actively goes after opportunities to make the homeworker feel both recognised and included.

Undoubtedly, increased homeworking brings new challenges to those responsible for driving employee engagement. Business leaders should take heart however, from research that found that homeworkers generally do more than their contracted hours, suffer lower levels of stress and get more done.[33]

The following activities are all key to maintaining high levels of engagement from homeworkers :

Employee Onboarding – for anyone recruited and likely to work a good deal from home onboarding becomes a time of special significance. It's the best opportunity for existing staff to get to know quickly a new face before they head off into the world of remote working. These first few days should include practices and exercises that facilitate introductions and the forming of quick, strong, working relationships. See one example from Legal Island "The E-bay Challenge" set out on p86;

Technical issues – remember for a homeworker both seeing and hearing a person still counts for a lot. Always

---

33   "Home is where the work is: A new study of homeworking in ACAS – and beyond", p14, 2013, Beauregard, Basile, Canonico (LSE Enterprise)

make sure that online meetings make the best use of the technology available (often for free) such as Zoom, Skype and Teams. The equipment doesn't need to be state-of-the-art but it does need to be fully functional. It will irritate the homeworker enormously not to mention colleagues if images freeze and voices distort because the supporting hardware or Wi-Fi connection is dated and unable to deliver what's needed;

Measure output not activity – yes you can install software that tracks time spent at a laptop or PC but it's far better to work off systems that measure output and performance rather than activity. Don't forget for homeworking to succeed there has to be a minimum level of trust between the two parties;

Recognition – the importance of recognition for home workers cannot be overstated. Out of sight shouldn't mean out of mind. Small gifts from Amazon focused on the homeworkers workspace could work well but don't forget the power of direct contact and a well done and thank you delivered personally over the phone;

Keep communication strong – if in doubt it's better to err on the side of too much communication rather than too little. Weekly schedules should set in stone time for 1-2-1s with managers and for teams to meet online and to share progress reports;

Protect career paths – it's important for homeworkers to know that their lack of physical presence in the office will not adversely affect their career prospects. Be sure never to confuse absence in the office with an absence

of ambition. Offer the same opportunities to all staff irrespective of where they choose to perform most of their work;

Clarify goals – any period of home working should be preceded by a clear conversation in terms of personal and company goals. What does the employee expect to achieve with this new method of working? What are the benefits but also the pitfalls that may have to be addressed? What plans does the employee have to confront these?;

Out of work activities – isolation remains one of the biggest challenges to business leaders looking to maintain the morale of homeworkers. This can be addressed by giving employees access to online chat facilities, planning into the weekly schedule time by the virtual water cooler and introducing individual or team games that can be played online such as fantasy football or virtual trading. Don't forget too the importance of meeting up in the real world. Old style meet-ups become particularly relevant to those who spend most of their time looking at colleagues through the medium of technology;

Time and boundary management – most homeworkers will have designated working hours and this should be respected by everyone. Last minute requests for work that will drive them outside of their standard hours should be avoided. So too should the random business idea dispatched over a weekend which could be communicated with equal effect at the beginning of the working week. Quality downtime is essential for all workers where they can be free from the influence of social media, online and business messages dropping in by email or text.

Barry Phillips

*From Start-Up to Platinum Employer – Five Key
Business Lessons*

This year we're celebrating our 21st anniversary and we're
often asked what we have learnt on our journey to where
we are now.

I've listed our big five key learning points below.

Lesson One: Get out of the Business Early

It's commonly said that when you start a business, you
have to go "all-in". You have to sacrifice everything else to
make sure you give it your very best, so the business has
the best chance of getting over the starting line.

I remember doing just this for at least the first five years
of Legal Island. When we eventually graduated from
homeworking to a bricks and mortar office, there were

very few days in which I left my desk before 10pm, having started at 7 that morning. I was in most weekends for at least one day; often both days. To this day, I have vivid memories of exiting the office with little energy left, dragging my feet across the car park to my car like a zombie with no other care in the world other than total commitment to one thing: the company, my company.

But when I look back at this now, I wonder whether much of this behaviour was really down to my needing a comfort blanket in the event it all went pear shaped. I wanted the security of saying to myself, 'If this business goes belly up, it's not going to be because I didn't work hard enough and throw everything I had at it'. But I realise now, with the benefit of hindsight, that when all you have in your tool shed is more hours, there's something badly wrong. It's more craft you need usually, not graft.

I think an entrepreneur's base position should be to aim to outthink and not outwork the opposition. From day one, they should ask, 'How can I do what I plan to do more cleverly than anyone else?' The opportunities to do this are unbounded. You need to make better quality decisions than your competitors and to resource and leverage better. Do these things and you'll steal a huge march on your competitors; and you'll enjoy lots more down time than them too.

Sure, there were times when we were punching well above our weight and having to meet impossible deadlines. We'd meet customers and they'd ask whether we had 20 or 30 staff. They'd then be shocked when they learned we had just five. But I'm sure that if I had given myself more finite working hours, I could have achieved much the same results or perhaps even better ones, because it would have forced me to work more intelligently.

In the seminal work, *The E-Myth,* Michael E Gerber talks about the importance of working *on* the business and not *in* it. Build a company based on systems, not one individual, he argues. Build your first business as though you plan to franchise it and document every process. Examples he quotes include McDonald's – probably the most successful franchising business in history. What I failed to do was lift myself out of the business early enough and Legal Island only really began to grow once I had managed to do this.

Lesson Two: How You Make and Review Decisions Is Critical. Make Time to Do Both of These Well.

I'm not from an entrepreneurial family. In fact, there are no entrepreneurs in my immediate family at all, although I've always felt my only sibling, Wendy, would make a good one if she gave it a go. None of my close friends are entrepreneurs. They work in the public sector or for banks or charities. Whilst I trust their advice, there are times in which you do need to speak to other entrepreneurs to bounce ideas off them, or to get them to test your strategising.

As Legal Island began to grow, I set up a senior team in the hope that they would assist me with high level thinking. Whilst it is important to consult colleagues on certain issues, I soon learnt this wasn't the mechanism

I needed to really draw out my big thinking. Often, you can't talk openly to colleagues about big plans because they may realise that the direction you have in mind may not include them, or at least it may not be good for them. There is also the issue of safety to speak. However approachable and amiable you are as a leader, it's unrealistic for you to expect them to really go at you when they think you've got something badly wrong. Also, any developing business necessarily needs a lot of administrators and implementor finishers. These people are vital to a business but they're not the sort that are best placed to help you with the big picture stuff; nor are they likely to encourage you to take the risk that you need to move a business to the next level.

Eventually, I decided to bite the bullet and set up a mechanism that was external to the business precisely for this purpose. The Legal Island Advisory Board proved to have the following benefits:

- I could cherry pick the people I felt had the experience I needed to help me make important business decisions;
- I could select those I felt would have the courage to challenge me and tell me plainly when they thought I was wrong;
- I could select people from backgrounds that would really enrich the decision-making process, and I made sure I did so. Our current board consists of two entrepreneurs, a process person and a business consultant.

The Legal Island Advisory Board usually meets three to four times a year for three hours each meeting. It helps with whatever we feel is needed, including strategy development, governance issues, contingency planning and, more recently, Brexit readiness.

I soon learnt that making business decisions is not only about having good people around you to consult. It's also about positioning yourself in such a way that you give yourself the best chance of making the best decision possible at that time.

Abraham Lincoln used to say that he aspired to be able to make decisions devoid of all pride, ego, bitterness and negativity. In the fabulous book, *Team of Rivals* by Doris Kearns Goodwin, the author describes how Lincoln appointed his cabinet purely on the basis of their fitness for the role. His own view of each and any rivalry or history shared between them and him appeared to play no part in the decision-making process in terms of who was appointed and who was not.

Einstein once said if I had one hour to resolve a challenge, I'd spend 55 minutes making sure I had asked the right questions, and the last five minutes working on the answer. Having read this, I now tend to ask myself a number of questions before making a big decision. These include the following:

1. Am I making this decision in this way simply to be consistent with an earlier decision? Is now the right time to actually admit that the first decision was wrong?;
There's no harm in doing this sometimes. I actually think this is good leadership;

2. Am I making this decision too early and working off a hunch that actually requires more research and evidence?;

3. Am I actually avoiding making a decision here because I feel I don't have enough evidence in front of me?

   To a point, this is in slight contradiction to question 2 above. It is important, however, to remember that we never operate with perfect information and knowledge, and at various points, you do have to work off hunches and gut feeling. Sometimes, refusing to make a decision because you're confronted with too many unknowns can be fatal. In the excellent book and film "Touching the Void," two climbers get in trouble whilst coming down from a snow-capped mountain in South America. One falls down a crevasse and breaks a leg. He's too weak to climb back up, but he doesn't know what lies further down inside the crevasse. What he does know is that a decision to do nothing and wait there will kill him. He lowers himself deep into the crevasse, knowing full well that he can't climb back out. Eventually, he sees a chink of light to one side, heads towards it and crawls out and back to base camp, saving his life.

4. Finally, is my head in the right place to make this decision right now? Am I feeling anger, frustration, fatigue or any other negative emotion that might skew this decision in the wrong direction?

Incidentally, I've found that an invaluable tool in this space is meditation. I meditate for at least ten minutes every day. It's amazing how many people rely on their brains as a principle means of making a living and yet do so little work on their brains themselves.

How you review your decision-making is another vital consideration. There are many factors that get in the way of thorough and objective analysis of a decision. Confirmation bias is one. Business leaders are very good at looking for evidence to support an existing view of something, rather than seeking out accurate explanations of what really happened. Moreover, the pace of business life is so fast that we rarely slow down enough to examine the series of decisions and activities that led to a given outcome. Instead, over time, business fables tend to show themselves. An outcome is said to have failed for one main reason which, when repeated enough or left without challenge, becomes the accepted explanation. The reality is that business ventures fail for many reasons and it's rarely because of one reason, such as a recession, an overpriced product or a poor distribution channel.

So many business books talk about the value of failure. Many podcast hosts ask interviewees about their favourite failure that actually propelled them to greater success, but I wonder if our obsession with failure is unhealthy, and that failure is overrated because we simply don't understand what really causes it in the first place. A while ago, we organised a number of events in London and Manchester. They didn't prove to be a great success. There was a team of about five people involved and if you were to ask any one of them today why we weren't more successful, my guess would be that you'd get several different answers.

Lesson Three: Understand How You Need to Network Changes as Your Business Develops.

It was Jim Rohn who said, 'You become the average of the five people you spend most of your time with'. I think about this a lot and wish I had been far more strategic in targeting and spending time with people relevant to my business world and development. I should have actively gone after people who were much further ahead of me in terms of their business journey. I should have read a lot more too, from those who had clearly succeeded and were sharing with others what they had spent a lot of time working out or finding out for themselves.

When Jim Rohn first came up with the quote, he likely meant that you should surround yourself physically with five important go-getters by joining the right social clubs, and attending the right business meetings and leadership events. Today, you can do it in an altogether different way. You can follow big hitters on Twitter, listen to their podcasts, or have one-on-one coaching sessions over Skype with a high level business leader anywhere in the world and one who you couldn't have hoped to have had access to a decade ago. In short, it's a lot easier to develop business skills with the help of others than it was before and there's no excuse not to.

The UK is crammed full of business networking events, from free breakfast seminars to black tie events costing a thousand pounds a table. Over the years, my attitude to networking has changed – or maybe my needs have. Either way, I approach networking very differently from before. In days gone by, I'd accept invitations to different events with no networking strategy in mind. I guess it was a classic case of FOMO. I was there for Fear of Missing Out by not being there. Now, I try instead to practise JOMO: The Joy of Missing Out when invited to attend something that has no relevance to me or the business. When something is on that I could otherwise have been at, I think of the quality time I'm having with family or the really good biography I'm reading, when I could have been standing with a glass of red wine while listening to someone moan about Brexit. I repeatedly ask myself before deciding to attend an event "Do I really need to be at this? And what's the opportunity cost to me of attending this?"

I'm not sure how much I get out of networking via the medium of social media too – or maybe here too, my needs are just changing. Certainly, in the early days of social media, applications like Twitter offered the opportunity for you to follow those you really rated to see what they were doing and to learn from them. LinkedIn appeared to be a great way to contact others with the expertise you needed to access. Today, many social media posts seem to be all about self-promotion with people declaring how delighted they are to be attending a particular event. Well, John Brown, I'm delighted that you're delighted, but where does this delight get us all? I'd feel better if I didn't see the vertical pronoun "I" so often in LinkedIn posts. And as for Facebook posts, there's so much social peacocking going on that it's almost unbearable to use now – and please don't get me started on those who use it to have conversations with partners that they should really be keeping for the home. On Valentine's Day, if you love her, tell her face to face! Or am I missing something here?

What's clear to me is that the very large majority of real movers and shakers in the UK aren't on social media at all. They are far too busy doing stuff to worry about representing themselves to others online. These others only seem to be watching because they've nothing much else to do anyway, or because they're seeking some sort of validation by engaging others in conversation about nothing of any real value or importance.

I still do attend the occasional networking event, mind you. If truth be told, I never know which version of me is going to turn up. Sometimes, it's the cynical Barry Phillips, who immediately questions what he's doing there. Most of the time, however, I try to maximise the time I've allocated to the exercise. Very occasionally, I really work a room and make loads of useful introductions. Over the years, I've learned a few tips for how to network well.

First and foremost, talk away from home. Put the spotlight on the person you're meeting and try to work out a way to help them. Helping others is the best way to network. Do a good turn for someone and it'll come back to you sometime in the future, and hey; if it never does, isn't it nice just to do good things for people anyway?

Secondly, take a genuine interest in the person you're meeting and talking to. Tony Robbins would say that if you're bored talking to someone, it's your own fault. I'm not sure if I totally agree with him, but in any ten-minute encounter with a complete stranger, a good networker should be able to find a person's sweet spot and get them to share and to talk about what really matters to them.

Thirdly, go armed with ready-to-use openers. A poor uphill start is difficult to recover from, but a strong opening helps tremendously. I use, "What's your interest in coming here?" or "What are your biggest challenges in business at the moment?" These are two very open questions that allow people to speak about whatever is most important to them at the time.

Lesson Four: Your Own Personal Development Is Critical. It's Important You Make Time for This

I truly believe we're in the golden age of audio now, and I use it a lot for my professional development. I listen to podcasts a great deal whilst cycling to and from work, shopping or doing other mundane activities.

A favourite podcast of mine is The Tim Ferriss Show. This is first-rate for two reasons. Firstly, the quality of people he gets on the show. It seems that no-one is beyond his reach. Secondly, the quality of his questions. He really does seem to be able to ask the questions that you really want to hear asked. Many reveal the complexity of business decision-making. Ferriss, of course, is also known for his books and his seminal work, "The Four-Hour Work Week". His more recent works, "Tools of Titans" and "Tribe of Mentors" are essential reading for anyone wanting to find out why certain leaders across many disciplines succeed.

I've already mentioned "The E-Myth" and just how important that book was for me. Two others that really made an impact were written by chess champions. Now don't get me wrong: my chess ability is limited to a knowledge of how each piece moves. If I showed you how to castle, you'd probably tell me it was wrong. But for me, the books take the learning from the game and illustrate well how you can apply it to life in general – but also, and more specifically, the business world. The first book is "How Life Imitates Chess" by Gary Kasparov.

I met Kasparov in London several years ago. He had the most penetrating eyes and stare I think I've ever seen, and he must have scared the living daylights out of many opponents across the chess board. In his book, Kasparov spends a lot of time talking about understanding the difference between tactics and strategy. He was so difficult to beat because he could change both at will. Tactics, he explains, is deciding whether to lead with your pawns or some of your second-row pieces. Strategy, on the other hand, is deciding whether to play aggressively or defensively, or to switch between the two in a game of two halves. He beat some of the greatest players in the history of chess by taking the type of game to the board that he knew they'd struggle with most.

The second chess book that is definitely worth a read is "The Art of Learning," by Josh Waitzkin. As well as being a world chess champion, he was a world champion martial arts expert in what is called Tai Chi, or sometimes "Push Hands". The book is about how he went after excellence and achieved it in both disciplines. He makes a very clear connection between the two sports, arguing that both rely heavily on drawing your opponent into making mistakes and, hopefully, fatal errors.

His book offers a huge amount in terms of how to be in the moment and how to set yourself up for optimum performance in whatever it is you do. There's a fabulous video on YouTube of his fight for a world title in Taiwan, which was obviously rigged in favour of his local opponent. It shows him clearly keeping his focus to beat his adversary while everyone around him was falling apart, complaining about the judging of the fight. To access this go to YouTube and search for Josh Waitzkin vs The Buffalo 2004.

But what he has to say about helping children to learn is insightful. He argues with some force that you should aim to praise effort, not success. As soon as you convince a child that he or she is naturally gifted at something, they are likely to quit the moment they experience failure. The drop is far too high. Help them understand, he says, that there is a learning process they can engage in, which will take them to excellence. This is the biggest gift you can give to children and their education. It is learning that will help them in the workplace too.

Lesson Five: Choose Your Business Partners with Great Care

Partnering up when you're an SME, particularly a micro-company, is a great way to punch above your weight and grow organically and quickly. Sometimes, you can identify a market need, but you can't satisfy it because you only have 50% of the required resources. Alternatively, it may be that you can satisfy the market 100%, but you just can't get to it because you don't have the access or the financial clout to pay for a marketing campaign that would get you there. In these cases, and many others, it makes sense to partner up and see if you can get to a win-win with an organisation that has mutual but not overlapping interest.

For me, early experiences of partnering up were rather mixed. A positive experience came when we partnered up with the training company Parity as early as 2003. We had access to a lot of people that they wanted to get in front of, and they had a supply of trainers that we could use for an event on people management. The result was a full-day skillsfest at the Waterfront in Belfast, that we jointly organised. It started at 9am and offered attendees a vast array of side-by-side seminars and workshops on people skills that they could pick and choose, right until it finished at 5pm. I can't remember how many trainers and sessions were offered side by side that day, but it was an event the likes of which I don't think Northern Ireland had seen until then – and I haven't seen much like it since. It was a superb day of learning and something neither party could have achieved on its own.

On the other hand, right down the other end was a partnership that I really would like to forget. We teamed up with a software company who was targeting the legal market. The agreement was that we would jointly host a seminar which Legal Island would market and administer, in return for them covering the cost of the venue and providing one of the two speakers. In our initial meeting, I had talked about the importance of the customer experience and the fact that a gentle sell was crucial so as not to damage the customer relationship, and they had agreed. I expressly mentioned that there should be no hard sell to delegates. So far, so good.

When I arrived at the venue, I noticed that two of their sales team were standing at the top of the hotel stairs, stopping every attendee from going any further until they had taken their details and asked them for a time for them to call and demo their software. I could see some of the delegates looking quite annoyed by this, and I was too. I found their team leader, who was also the guy I had formed the partnership with and pointed out politely what his sales team were doing – and that I felt it was too pushy. He promptly replied, "Barry, we've paid good money to be here and we need to get full value". Then, he immediately walked off in the other direction. Maybe they did get value; maybe they didn't, but they got no further value from our relationship. We did nothing with them after that. That company, incidentally, is no longer in existence.

Vetting Partners

Working out whether a business might have an interest in partnering up with you is one thing; but assessing whether that partnership is likely to work and get you both to a better place is quite another. How do you do it? If you approach them, the chances are that it's because you've seen what they do and are familiar with their reputation. But sometimes companies approach you out of the blue and you have to decide whether it's a green, amber or red light you have to show them.

You can ask them for an indication of the kitemarks they have, which should give you an idea as to how well-organised or governed the company is, and how well it treats and manages its staff. But if you request too much, there's a danger that the other party will feel like they're in some sort of tender process. As two companies size each other up, there's a lot of ego floating around and one request that is deemed to be out of place could do an inordinate amount of damage.

One useful tip is this. Before entering into a major partnership agreement, give them a simple task or mini-project to deliver on first. A few years back, I was approached by the founder of a company with a view to partnering up on some interesting R&D projects that they were bringing to fruition. He was clearly a clever guy and struck me as someone likely to make a lot of money at some point in his life. But I had my reservations too. Was he someone who liked to make promises that those behind him just wouldn't be able to keep? I suspected he may be.

We diarised a second meeting for about a month in the future. In the mean time I asked if he could source a few documents from his company for us that we had discussed in the meeting and then provide us with online access to view their beta products. He said he'd have them to me inside a week. Three weeks later, nothing had been sent. I only heard from him again when he called, wanting to know why I had cancelled our next meeting.

APPENDICES

Many of the documents in the Appendices can be found
and downloaded online at :

employeeengementresources.net

Barry Phillips and Jayne Gallagher regularly speak or chair at conferences on business and employment topics. They also offer coaching and mentoring sessions to individuals and SMEs.

For more information contact:

businesssupport@legal-island.com

Legal Island – Here's the Deal

Introduction

Legal Island is a trusted, world class provider of quality legal information and training. Established in 1998 the company has enjoyed phenomenal growth and market penetration. Each year, we continue to set new standards for the services we deliver which are unrivalled by our competitors. We are now used by a large majority of the top 500 companies in Northern Ireland the Republic of Ireland.

Due to our ambitious plans for growth we are looking for more talented people to join our team. We'd like you to join us if we suit you and you suit us. What follows is our attempt to describe ourselves to you. Please read what follows carefully. It is vitally important that you understand who we are and what we are about.

What We Can Offer You

- 2004: Winner of the Invest NI Award Best use of the Internet by a Company in NI
- 2007: Winner of the *Irish News* Awards Best Place to Work Award
- 2008: Recruited 12 new staff & moved to new and much larger premises
- 2009: Partnership with *The Belfast Telegraph* to bring new subjects to new audiences in Northern Ireland
- 2009: Winner of the *Irish News* Workplace & Employment, Innovative Employer Award
- 2009: Winner of the *Irish News* Workplace & Employment, Best Place to Work Award
- 2009: Accredited with Investors in People Award
- 2010: Highly Commended at the *Irish News* Workplace & Employment Awards, Managing Talent
- 2010: Highly Commended at the *Irish News* Workplace & Employment Awards, Best Place to Work
- 2010: Highly Commended at the *Irish News* Workplace & Employment Awards, Innovative Employer
- 2011: EFQM Mark of Excellence Award
- 2011: MD Finalist of Young Businesswomen of the Year Award (WIB Awards)
- 2012: Gold Star Customer Service Award – EFQM
- 2013: Accredited with Bronze Investors in People
- 2013: Winners of Employers for Childcare Awards Small Medium Enterprise Category
- 2014: Accredited with Gold Investors in People
- 2014: Accredited with ISO9001
- 2015: Shortlisted for BITC Employer of Choice
- 2016: Reaccredited with ISO9001
- 2017: Reaccredited with Gold Investors in People

- 2019: Accredited with Platinum Investors in People

Our winning entries in various award categories highlight and note that Legal Island staff enjoy the following benefits with us:

- A competitive salary and package
- Opportunity for learning and development
- Payment & time off for training in CIPD or management qualifications
- Assistance with objective setting to help devise personal development plans
- Opportunities for flexible working to suit the needs of individual workers
- The opportunity to try things a little bit different or challenging.
- One-to-One coaching – almost all staff have attended or currently are attending coaching sessions with some of Northern Ireland's top performance coaches. Our managers have all been trained to be coaches, too.

What We Expect in Return

- Hard work! We play hard. We work hard!
- Commitment to the company ethos of constant development. This means that when you are with us you will be constantly striving to improve and develop yourself.
- Commitment to the company's Employee Principles, Staff Charter, Values and Culture.
- A positive can-do-will-give-it-my-best attitude. We need people who are prepared to try at this company –

those who will give a task their best effort every time.

- Ownership – however junior or senior your work with us we expect you to enjoy taking real ownership of what you do. You should understand that your job and tasks evolve and it is for you to constantly strive to improve the way you work and how tasks may be executed.
- Innovation & Creativity – we want all our people to be innovative and creative in completing tasks. They should be results-focused and see challenges not problems and ways to overcome obstacles.
- Ideas and Networking – Legal Island relies on its staff for new ideas and innovation. All staff are expected to contribute to the process of devising new projects, new services or simply better ways of executing tasks. The same applies to networking and sourcing leads and resources for the company.

"Our Staff Matter, Legal Island Cares – A Shared Commitment"

Legal Island is committed to creating a culture where staff are valued and supported by managers and colleagues. As a company we support a culture of openness and mutual respect in which a healthy work life balance can be achieved in an environment where all staff can develop to their full potential.

Colleagues at Legal Island will be encouraged to play as full a part as they can in the life, goals and culture of the company. As part of our commitment to you we have adopted our Staff Charter. This staff charter is part of

Legal Island's commitment to you as an employee, but we acknowledge that it forms only part of that commitment. As an employee you also have a set of responsibilities to the organisation, your colleagues and our customers.

1. Our Promise to You

As an employer, we want all our staff to feel valued by being involved, and given appropriate development opportunities within a diverse, stimulating and innovative working environment.

Our Commitment to You...

- You will be involved in setting the goals and objectives of Legal Island
- You will understand how staff roles contribute towards achieving our goals and objectives
- You will share in and contribute to the wider benefits of Legal Island life

What we expect from You...

- Contribute to establishing the goals and objectives of Legal Island and work towards achieving them
- Contribute as appropriate to the wider life of Legal Island
- Work towards ensuring that the customer is at the centre of everything we do
- Work outside of your comfort zone from time to time and regularly in your "stretch zone"
- Help Legal Island establish the highest standards of customer care

2. Leadership and Management

Legal Island strives to provide the most effective management and leadership to enhance working relationships, at all levels, on the basis of trust.

Our management style demonstrates leadership and accountability and promotes an ethos and image that positively reflects the company's commitment to equal opportunities.

The role of the manager requires an engagement with new ways of working, dealing with new competition, embracing new technologies and understanding the culture of the company. As the business environment changes, managers need to be responsible, flexible and seek new ways of working.

Our Commitment to You...

• We will provide a clear sense of direction – which will be communicated on a regular basis
• We will provide appropriate levels of support and supervision; showing encouragement and recognition
• We will draw on staff creativity and innovation wherever possible
• Managers will embody and promote the values of the Staff Charter
• We will invest in the professional development of all staff

Staff are expected to...

• Act with integrity and trustworthiness and be accountable for their professional conduct

- Contribute to the building of good working relationships; work cooperatively with and support managers and colleagues
- Contribute to an effective team working environment
- Embrace the Staff Charter and behave within the spirit of it
- Seek to resolve issues and problems at work constructively and efficiently, showing dignity and respect to others

3. Communication and Staff Involvement

Legal Island recognises good two-way communication can support an environment where employees feel valued and where contributions are recognised. Engaged staff have the opportunity for upward feedback and feel well-informed about what is happening in the company. We associate a climate of involvement and consultation with employee satisfaction and commitment, promoting better performance and satisfaction in your working life.

We will encourage feedback from staff on communication and involvement, so that we can find new and more effective ways of achieving this goal.

Our Commitment to You...

- We will create individual and company objectives that are realistic and challenging
- We will provide constructive and effective feedback and appraisal, together with formal and informal support and information
- We will support staff effectively in their roles

- We will have regular progress reviews with staff
- We will recognise and value staff achievements
- We will encourage and maintain a positive working environment

Staff are expected to...

- Be responsible for reviewing and analysing their own performance and fully completing performance review documents in the time specified
- Actively seek to improve their performance and maintain an innovative approach to where appropriate
- Contribute to planning and objective setting
- Seek and respond to feedback
- Keep their line manager informed on the progress of their work and any issues that may arise

4. Personal and Organisational Development

Legal Island regards the development of its workforce as critical to its development and success and aims to create and sustain a supportive working environment which will nurture personal development and organisational development. We will achieve this by ensuring that what we do is relevant to current and future needs in order to respond to new opportunities and challenges.

Staff at Legal Island will be encouraged to realise their full potential in their job role and continue their personal and professional development. Legal Island provides training periods for staff development. All staff must participate in the training and development relevant to the organisational needs.

Our Commitment to You...

- To provide an effective welcome and induction when joining the organisation
- To receive information on training and development opportunities relevant to each individual staff member and the goals and objectives of the organisation
- To conduct regular performance reviews
- Provide a culture of learning and personal development including coaching and mentoring

Staff are expected to...

- Take responsibility for their own ongoing learning and development and provide feedback on training
- Participate actively in induction and training sessions
- Develop skills and knowledge in their current role and be flexible in the face of future changes or challenges
- Use their experience and skills to help others learn
- Be proactive in their work and actively challenge current processes to highlight ways in which we could do them better
- Constantly strive to improve themselves and develop as a person

5. Dignity at Work

Legal Island is committed to providing equal opportunity in employment and avoiding unlawful discrimination in employment or to staff and customers, striving to ensure that the work environment is free from harassment and bullying and that everyone is treated with dignity and respect.

Our Commitment to You...

- To treat all staff with respect and trust
- To actively promote diversity and equality
- Not to disadvantage by disability, sex, gender reassignment, pregnancy, colour, race, nationality, ethnic or national origins, sexual orientation or religion or belief, age, employment status, social background or because someone is married or is a civil partner or any other irrelevant distinction

Staff are expected to...

- Show courtesy and respect to everyone with whom they come into contact
- Act in ways free from prejudice and stereotypical assumptions
- Act on sensitivities about language and actions that may offend
- Value difference and the opportunity to share knowledge and skills in a diverse workplace.

6. Health and Safety at Work

Legal Island is committed to ensuring, so far as is reasonable practicable, the health, safety and welfare of their employees at work. We will aim to provide the necessary health, safety and welfare services for the well-being of all Legal Island employees.

Our Commitment to You...

- Health and Safety Policies to be actively communicated

- Access to information and appropriate forms of support
- To be treated with understanding and sensitivity when ill and to be supported on their return to work
- To provide a qualified first aid staff member

Staff are expected to...

- Promote their own health and safety procedures and report ill-health absences in line with company procedure
- Promote their own health and well-being and take their full holiday entitlement
- Refrain from working an excessive number of hours a week (manage their time effectively)

7. Employees and Each Other

Staff are expected to...

- Be loyal to absent colleagues, including ex-colleagues
- Respect individual opinion
- Value openness, truthfulness and honesty between colleagues
- Respect others by listening, acknowledging and responding
- Value the importance of strong and clear communication with colleagues
- Be responsible for working safely and ensuring the safety of other

Legal Island Employee Principles

Legal-Island Staff aspire to:

- Be respectful
- Be tolerant
- Be supportive and approachable
- Show integrity and trust
- Understand
- Consider their impact on others
- Practice what they preach.

The sign below can be found on the walls of our office.

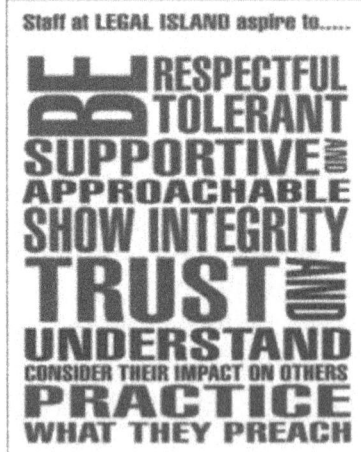

APPENDIX 2

Total Reward Statement

NAME OF EMPLOYEE

The following section provides details of the benefits that, in addition to your basic salary, make up your Total Reward Package. The information is based on your benefits for 2018-19 and your closing salary as at 31.07.19.

Breakdown:

Annual Salary Based on FT/ PT XX Hour Week	£
Bonuses	£

Pay and Benefits	**Provider and Benefit Level**	**Company Contribution**
Pension	Aegeon	£
Dividends		£
Medical Insurance + Critical Illness Cover	AXA PPP Healthcare	£
Employee Assistance Programme	Westfield Health Package	£

*National Insurance Contributions   £

Additional benefits:
• Paid time off to attend medical appointments (up to 2 hours) • Learning and Development Training (2 weeks annually) • Discounts and savings through Westfield Rewards https://   westfieldrewards.co.uk/ • Consideration of unpaid leave for extended breaks

Total Reward Package:

Annual Salary Based on FT/ PT XX Hour Week	£
Bonuses	£
Benefits	£
Total Reward Package	£

Breakdown of Leave

Paid Leave	Hours	Hourly Rate	Cost
Statutory Leave			
Additional Contractual Leave			
Long Service Addition			
Birthday Leave			
Total Contractual Leave			
Sick Leave (Prior to SSP)			
Time off on SSP			
Study Leave			
Compassionate Leave			
Total Paid Leave			

DATE

Dear

RE: Total Rewards Statement for End of Financial Year XXXX

We are pleased to present you with your personalised Total Reward Statement for for the financial year to XXXX.

Your Total Reward Statement provides you with a summary of your overall remuneration and gives you an overview of the investment that we make in your reward.

Your statement includes your annual salary and bonus figures, and your annualised benefits based on your 2018-2019 package. We have also included your salary as of XXXXX at the end of the Statement.

Also included in your statement is a summary of the benefits that are made available to you.

We do hope that you will find this a useful tool in reviewing your overall package but if you have any questions, please feel free to contact XXXX or myself.

Thank you for your valuable contribution to our success in XXXXX

With best wishes

Jayne Gallagher

Managing Director

Legal Island

APPENDIX 3

Reward and Recognition

What Matters To You...

Reward & Recognition - What Matters To You...

Recognition is personal and how one person would like to be recognized for their contributions and achievements may be different from another. In order to assess the preferences of employees in our company, the Recognition Committee would like to know what matters to you. This information will help inform the creation of employee recognition activities. Please take a moment to complete this brief questionnaire. We will keep the survey private but we do ask that you complete all fields as it's a bit difficult to know what you like if you keep yourself anonymous!

Remember, it must not be forgotten that recognition and praise should not be a one off – a thank you or a well done any day of the week can make a huge difference and the point of the "What Matters To You" survey is not to determine what that one off "reward" might be it's to give your manager and colleagues a better idea of what motivates you.

1. Employee details:

Name:

2. I prefer to be recognized the following way: (check all that apply)

	Strongly Agree	Neither Agree nor Disagree	Strongly Disagree
Public praise (Monday Morning Meeting/ Staff meeting)	○	○	○
Private praise (one-on-one)	○	○	○
Thank you note/card	○	○	○
Thank you e-mail (personal)	○	○	○
Thank you e-mail (company-wide)	○	○	○

Other (please specify)

3. I most appreciate recognition when given by: (check all that apply)

	Strongly Agree	Neither Agree nor Disagree	Strongly Disagree
Peers	○	○	○
Managers	○	○	○
MD	○	○	○
CEO	○	○	○
No Preference	○	○	○

4. I prefer to be rewarded the following way: (check all that apply)

	Strongly Agree	Neither Agree nor Disagree	Strongly Disagree
Buns/Doughnuts/Ice cream afternoons etc	○	○	○
Opportunity to attend training of choice	○	○	○
Opportunity to participate on committees, projects	○	○	○

Remember, it must not be forgotten that recognition and praise should not be a one off – a thank you or a well done any day of the week can make a huge difference and the point of the "What Matters To You" survey is not to determine what that one off "reward" might be it's to give your manager and colleagues a better idea of what motivates you.

1. Employee details:

Name:

2. I prefer to be recognized the following way: (check all that apply)

	Strongly Agree	Neither Agree nor Disagree	Strongly Disagree
Public praise (Monday Morning Meeting/ Staff meeting)	O	O	O
Private praise (one-on-one)	O	O	O
Thank you note/card	O	O	O
Thank you e-mail (personal)	O	O	O
Thank you e-mail (company-wide)	O	O	O

Other (please specify)

3. I most appreciate recognition when given by: (check all that apply)

	Strongly Agree	Neither Agree nor Disagree	Strongly Disagree
Peers	O	O	O
Managers	O	O	O
MD	O	O	O
CEO	O	O	O
No Preference	O	O	O

4. I prefer to be rewarded the following way: (check all that apply)

	Strongly Agree	Neither Agree nor Disagree	Strongly Disagree
Buns/Doughnuts/Ice cream afternoons etc	O	O	O
Opportunity to attend training of choice	O	O	O
Opportunity to participate on committees, projects	O	O	O
Lunch outings	O	O	O
Cinema tickets	O	O	O
Vouchers	O	O	O
Time off	O	O	O

ie time to see a careers advisor etc	⌣	⌣	⌣
Extended lunch break	○	○	○
Flowers	○	○	○
Certificate	○	○	○
Book	○	○	○
Surprise	○	○	○

Other (please specify)

```
                                                          
```

5. My Favourite Things:

Sugary treat

Salty treat

Non-alcoholic beverage

Alcoholic beverage

Colour

Sports Team

Music

Hobby

Restaurant

Flowers

Other

6. What sort of innovative ways do you think we could record staff achievements?
e.g. staff board, social media

```

```

7. As a company we are always striving to ensure that our staff consistently perform well. There are times though when individuals go that extra mile and that too must be recognised.
In your opinion, what are the criteria you feel people should be recognised against for going the extra mile?

```

```

APPENDIX 4

New Start Checklist

Staff Member Name: _____

Start Date: _____

Duties	YES	NO	Additional
Equipment			
Desk			
Chair			
Bin			
Desk Drawers			
Desk Trays			
Suspension Folders			
Stationery			
Desk Tidy			
Paper Clips			
Post-its			
To do list			
Notebook			
Diary			
Calculator			
Stapler			
Staples			
Markers			
Name badge			
Business cards			
IT			
PC/Laptop			
Docking Station			
Keyboard			
Mouse			
Mouse Mat			
Printer set-up			
Email address			
Username and login details			
Company@			
Marketing@			
Finance@			
Shared point folder			
ESS Login details			
Outlook calendar-shared with all staff			
TELEPHONE			
Telephone handset			
Mobile			
Extension set up			
Telephone training			
Copy of extensions			

Meetings etiquette and expectations			
JAYNE Company strategy and info			
JAMES Payroll, Aviva, Westfield and Pension			

New Start Information Pack

You are very welcome to Legal Island.

USEFUL INFORMATION

Welcome _____ here is some information which you may find useful but please don't hesitate to ask if you have any questions or need any clarification.

IT

Your login details are as follows:

Login-
Password-
Email address-

If you wish to email all staff at once, you can use:

xxxxxx@Legal Island.com

If you have any IT problems you should email the Office Manager (ext 207) or email xxxxxx@Legal Island.com and she will pass the query onto the external IT technician.

Sharepoint

All folders and files are stored on the Share Point. Your folder is called _____ and you can store documents and folders in this. This is publicly viewed so all confidential information should be password protected.

To access the Sharepoint, carry out the following:

Login to your laptop/PC

Click on the yellow File Explorer Icon on the taskbar

Choose "Company-Shared"

Your PC is linked to the main printer in the office.

Clear Desk Policy

We operate a Clear Desk Policy in Legal Island whereby when you leave the office to go home, your desk should be cleared of all work related papers and folders. These papers and folders should be stored in the drawers and shelves around the office. The OM will forward you the link to this.

Work Desk Assessment

The Office Manager will carry out an initial assessment of your desk to ascertain any problems or issues with it and this will be arranged by her with you.

Evacuation Procedures

Fire Exits are situated at the back of the office downstairs and in the office upstairs. There are also 2 exits in the training centre. The Office Manager will carry out a Fire Drill twice yearly. Fire notices are situated in the kitchen and upstairs on the pillar and you should familiarise yourself with the procedure for spotting a fire.

Should the fire alarms go off you will hear a loud siren throughout the premises. It is advised that you leave immediately. We operate a buddy system for evacuations. The purpose of this is so that in the event of an evacuation, each person will know if their buddy is in or out of the office and can report this to the Office Manager at the assembly point on the roundabout. Your fire buddy is _____.

The Office Manager will also send you an online Fire Safety Course to complete, this is essential and you should let the OM know once you have completed it.

Telephones

The Customer Service Team is primarily responsible for answering incoming calls and in their absence other staff members should answer. It is LI policy that a call is answered within 3 rings.

Making Calls

To make an internal call lift receiver and dial the extension of the staff member required. To make an external call, left the receiver, dial 9 followed by the caller's number.

Mobile Phones

Mobile calls can be taken or made within reason and these can be answered in the storeroom or outside. If it is a lengthy call that you need to take or make this should be kept until outside working hours.

To avoid distracting other employees, it is best that these are not answered in the main office.

Dress Code

The dress code within the office is Smart Casual. If you have to attend an external meeting, you are expected to dress smartly and in a professional manner.

Behaviour and Conduct

As an employee of LI you are expected to adhere to the principles of the company and these are displayed on the walls in the office, both downstairs and upstairs.

Stationery

All items of stationery have been provided for you and there are additional items available in the downstairs stationery cupboard. Should there be any item you require, which isn't in the cupboard, just ask the Office Manager. Likewise, if you use the last of any item please tell the OM.

Annual Leave

The annual leave year runs from January-December. If you are part-time your a/l balance will be worked out on a pro-rata basis. Depending on the time of year that you are starting with us, you will also be given a pro-rata balance for annual leave. This will be sent to you by the OM. The most you can carry forward at the end of a year is 1 week, unless you have been given special permission by your line manager.

ESS Annual Leave System

All staff annual leave is processed through the ESS system. The Office Manager will send you through the login details for you to register and then she will approve your registration. Once you request annual leave it will be sent to _____ for approval. Days which need to be entered retrospectively can only be entered by your line manager.

Business Closure Days

LI will close on the 10 NI business closure days throughout the year. This does not affect your annual leave balance. If you are part-time your allowance for business closure days will be worked out on a pro-rata basis.

Christmas Leave

The office will be closed over the Christmas period- from 25th-1st inclusive. Therefore you should ensure you have enough days to cover the non- business closure days within this period (BC days- Christmas Day, Boxing Day and New Year's Day)

Birthday Leave

You have been allocated an extra day of leave in lieu of your birthday. This date should be out through on the ESS system, but it won't be deducted from your a/l balance.

Unable to come into work

If you are sick or unable to come into work, you should telephone your line manager before 9.30am to make them aware. If your line manager is not in the office, you should ask to speak to another manager. If you get delayed coming into work, you should contact your line manager to make her/him aware- this should be done in a safe manner. Full details of sick leave can be viewed in the policies, available in the Shared Point.

Meetings

During your time within LI, you will be part of many meetings. You should adhere to the following guidelines...

To clarify where necessary, what is required of you well in advance of any meeting;

•   To prepare well for all meetings;

- To circulate any substantial materials to which you plan to refer to in the meeting in good time;
- To turn up promptly for all meetings and be ready to contribute at all times;
- To study the agenda carefully - so you know when best to make what contributions;
- To ask questions if there is anything that you don't understand at meetings;
- To practice your listening skills when not directly concerned with a point on the agenda;
- To respect other people's views in the meeting, not interrupt or talk over others;
- To keep to the agenda and to do your best to keep contributions "on point" not "off point".

The meeting space available within the premises is as follows:

- Snug, upstairs
- Training Centre
- Barry's office, only when Barry is out of the office.
- Kitchen-time restrictions apply (unavailable-10.30am-11.30 and 12.30pm-2.30pm and 3pm-4pm)

You only need to book the training centre rooms and this can be done by emailing the Office Manager in plenty of time to allow for the heating to be set. .

Internet Usage

PCs and laptops are provided for the work of LI only and not for personal use. Any personal internet browsing should be kept to a minimum during work hours.

Outlook Calendar

All staff uses the Outlook calendar as a means of letting others know their whereabouts. An outlook calendar has been set up for you and all staff have accepted your calendar and shared their own with you. You have also been provided with a diary.

Kitchen

The kitchen is available for all staff to use for breaks and lunches. You are entitled to a 10 min break in the morning and afternoon. Lunch should be taken between 12noon and 2pm. Lunch food cannot be eaten at the desk as it is good for staff to eat with one another in the kitchen. Alternatively, you can leave the office to have your lunch.

All supplies and equipment in the kitchen is for you to use. The company provides tea, coffee, milk, sugar, butter and jam. You can use the fridge to store your food. Crockery and cutlery is there for your use as well although feel free to bring in your own cup.

Dietary Requirements/Intolerances

If you have any food allergies or specific dietary requirements, please make DK aware of this.

Medical Conditions

If you have any medical conditions that you feel we need to be made aware of, please inform you Line Manager or the Office Manager.

Pay Day

You will be paid on the 28th of the month. Should this date fall on a weekend or a bank holiday, you will be paid on the closest working day. At Christmas time you will be paid on an earlier date – to be confirmed by the Finance Manager.

Opening up/Locking up

All staff work various hours and the office is usually open from 8am to 5.30pm. The Office Manager will show you the opening and locking up procedures if you are required to open or lock up. You will be provided with a door fob and gate key and this should be kept safe.

Smoking

A smoking area is provided around the side of the building.

Health and Wellbeing

LI will run a number of health and wellbeing activities throughout the year. Information will be sent to you beforehand.

Car Parking

You can park anywhere in the carpark. When the training centre is being used, staff should park on the gravel car park or around the front.

Reward and Recognition

The OM has emailed you a survey to complete and the purpose of this is to determine what your likes and dislikes are in a number of areas.

Fleece and Polo shirt

A fleece been provided for you and this can be worn if you are helping to set up at an event.

Should you have any questions about any of these areas, please don't hesitate to speak to your line manager or to the Office Manager.

New Start Information

Please complete the following and return to the Office Manager

Personal Details

Full name: _____

Date of Birth: _____

Home Address _____

_____

_____

Postcode: _____

Telephone Number: _____

National Insurance Number: _____

Name of Next of Kin: _____

Relationship to You: _____

TelephonenumberforNextofkin:_____

Home address for Next of Kin:_____

_____

Are you happy for your Next of Kin to be your Emergency
Contact? YES/NO

Are you happy for us to securely store the details of your
Next of Kin? YES/NO

Dietary

Do you have any dietary requirements that we need to be
aware of? YES/NO

If yes, please detail below

_____

Medical

Do you have any medical conditions that you feel we need to be aware of? YES/NO

If yes, please detail _____

_____

_____

Private and Confidential   Ref No:

Employee Led Start, Stop, Continue, Change Exercise

This is a great way of getting feedback and ideas on what is happening in your business and indeed what your staff believe should be happening there too.

With this exercise you are looking to understand which activities your employees would like to see started, which items should be stopped, and which things should continue in their current form or with a slight change.

When done well it can be really powerful, unearthing many new ideas some of which may be small and easy to implement (like a new item for the staff kitchen for example) or be huge, such as an idea for a brand new income stream.

How do you do it?

You ask staff to get together in a room and give them shed loads of post-it notes. The notes should be placed at one of four locations marked "Start", "Stop", "Continue", "Change". These may be walls, flipcharts, tables etc.

It's usually best to do the exercise with the business leader/s out of the room in order that employees feel at their most comfortable.

Then What Happens?

The post-it notes are gathered up by the business leader/s who first look to bunch the notes into themes or categories. They then sift them into relevant piles: those ideas that can be acted on straight away (Quick wins – those fine two words...) those that may require more thought and resources and those ideas that should not be taken up.

What Can Possibly Go Wrong?

Two things actually and it's important for you to remember these if you have yet to do a SSCC exercise.

First, you deal with expectations at the start. Explain to staff that simply because something is mentioned (even by a majority of staff) it doesn't follow that you are bound to implement the idea. Promise instead, to give it due consideration and an explanation as to why you plan (or indeed don't plan) to act on it;

Second, you must follow up on the ideas posted. Give employees a date by which you will get back to them with you explanation in terms of what has and has not be acted on and why.

Remember there is something worse than not listening to staff. It is pretending to listen. It is crucial that within a reasonable time you respond to staff with your feedback on the points raised.

APPENDIX 7

Resolution Procedure

Please take independent legal advice before introducing this document into your business.

Objective

Most issues or problems at work are easily resolved through communication between employees and their colleagues or managers.

The objective of this Resolution Procedure is to help an employee resolve difficulties relating to a relationship at work with a colleague or with the company. It provides for difficulties to be addressed quickly and effectively and for resolutions to be made, where possible, at the earliest moment and as near as possible to the point of origin. The procedure establishes the appropriate steps to be followed when pursuing and dealing with a workplace issue.

INFORMAL PROCEDURE

It is preferable for all concerned that workplace difficulties are dealt with informally whenever possible. This is likely to produce solutions that are speedy, effective and minimise embarrassment and the risk of breaching confidentiality. This informal approach in no way proposes to diminish the issue or the effect it may have on individuals. The objective of the Informal Procedure is to allow scope for resolving issues quickly and with the minimum of distress.

In the first instance an employee who believes that they are experiencing a workplace difficulty relating to another member of the staff should approach the person responsible and make them aware that the behaviour is unwelcome or offensive and ask them to stop. Many incidents may be dealt with effectively in this manner as often the person responsible is unaware of the effect her/ his behaviour is having on others and will cease these actions on being made aware of the distress caused by them. An employee can seek the advice and support of another person, including a trade union representative, if they wish.

If the employee does not feel comfortable in approaching the relevant person directly, he or she can seek the support of their Line Manager in doing so. The Line Manager should attempt to facilitate a resolution of the matter. This may involve the Line Manager facilitating an informal discussion between the two employees. Often an informal discussion is enough to alert a person to the effects of her or his behaviour and can lead to greater understanding and an agreement that the behaviour will stop.

The types of informal resolution that could result may include an apology from the person against whom the complaint was made or an agreement that the conduct or behaviour will not be repeated. It might simply be an explanation to the complainant about what occurred from the point of view of the person against whom the complaint has been made which dispels the complaint. The Line Manager should keep a record of the complaint, a record of any meetings and decisions or agreements reached. The HR Manager is available to provide assistance.

It is recognised that circumstances may occasionally exist where, for good reasons, an employee cannot pursue her/his complaint through his/her own line management structure. In such circumstances, the complainant may bring her/his case to a higher level manager, or directly to the HR Manager, or equivalent, if appropriate. S/he will, if appropriate, initially seek to resolve the matter informally with the consent of the parties involved.

If the Informal Procedure has been attempted but the problem persists then the complaint can be dealt with either by Mediation or through the Formal Procedure.

MEDIATION

Mediation is a voluntary process for resolving disputes whereby a neutral and impartial person facilitates the parties in a dispute to explore the area(s) of dispute and, where possible, to assist them in reaching a mutually acceptable agreement/settlement.

Where it is considered that a complaint may be resolved by Mediation, or a complainant specifically requests Mediation, the Line Manager or HR Manager will write to both parties offering them the opportunity to take part in Mediation and outlining the procedures for Mediation.

When an offer of Mediation has been sent to the complainant and the subject of the complaint, they will be asked to indicate if they object to participating in Mediation. If no objection is received within five working days from either party, the Line Manager or HR Manager will appoint an independent Mediator to handle the Mediation. A mutually convenient time will be arranged for the Mediation to take place with the aim that the mediation takes place within another five working days.

If either the complainant or the subject of the complaint would like to know more about Mediation and/or meet the Mediator(s) to talk about the Mediation process to help them decide if they will participate, this will be facilitated, through the HR Manager.

Where Mediation is unsuccessful or the offer(s) of Mediation is refused, the complainant or the HR Manager may commence the Formal Procedure. The possibility of Mediation should remain open to the parties at any stage.

An investigator appointed under the Formal Procedure may refer a matter under investigation to Mediation if requested to do so by the parties.

FORMAL PROCEDURE

The Formal Procedure may be followed if the matter is not resolved under the Informal Procedure or through Mediation.

MAKING A FORMAL COMPLAINT (FORMAL STAGE 1)

Drop in your formal complaint procedure here....

Legal Island's Top Ten Engagement Tools

In no particular order (for they're all good...)

Top Banana – recognising people who move us – at the end of each year we have special banana themed thank you cards made up which each staff member takes responsibility for sending to the external person (or people) who have really impacted on them during the previous 12 months. This can be a specialist who has collaborated on a project, a person who has mentored and inspired us or just someone who has made our life that bit easier and who we would like to thank.

Ebay Challenge – in a race against time new staff use their taste, judgment and £10 (supplied by the company) to buy an item or items from the local shops (one hour starting from... now). Once back with your booty you list it on Ebay to sell within seven days and aim to make as much profit as possible for the company charity.

Supporting Charities – we send out surveys to our delegates after each event and for each completed survey we donate £1/€1 to a staff nominated charity. To decide on our charity for the year every staff member is entitled to nominate one charity from Northern Ireland and one from the Republic of Ireland – this can be either a popular and well known charity, one that has had a direct impact on that staff member or a specialist local charity which may not have the recognition but which we think needs support. All staff vote and one is chosen from each jurisdiction – at the end of the year we have a cheque presentation ceremony.

Staff Days Out – these have ranged from walking gourmet tours to quiz days and outdoor challenges – a chance for staff to catch up with colleagues from other teams outside of work mode, break down silos and have fun!

Visiting Musicians – from Scottish Bag Pipers to Finnish accordion players we've just about had them all here.

Surprise, Surprise – really does live up to its name! The CEO gives out a cryptic clue and any staff member who wants to can put their name into the hat to be chosen at random. Ever been submerged in a seaweed bath, gone floating in a flotation tank, taken a tandem ride round town or foraged for food in local woodland? Well you can now!!!!!

Stand-up Meetings – with our favourite music every time – the number one from the date you were born, your favourite chart song or something that is in line with the meeting theme – it's always a surprise!

Treats on Us – free coffee from the visiting coffee van, free ice-cream from the specially dialled in ice-cream van; is it your birthday – each month we have birthday buns (and exotic fruit for those who prefer). Also the talented bakers amongst staff will treat everyone with homemade goodies in true Bake-Off style.

Visiting Experts – from nutritionists to charity leaders, the company makes full use of its wide network built up over the years to bring in experts and thought leaders for "chalk and talk", discussion sessions and one to one meetings. Sharing knowledge and paying it forward.

Stop, Start, Continue, Change – every year all staff get together and have the opportunity to tell the company what we think the we should stop, start, continue doing or indeed just change. The process has thrown out all sorts of ideas from a new type of coffee we should keep in the kitchen through to a major new business initiative.

APPENDIX 9

Twelve Books that Helped Make Legal Island

Many of the books below really transformed Legal Island. To the authors we are eternally grateful.

Happy at Work, Sophie Rowan
    Wisdom from a leading psychologist on how to find contentment at work
High Output Management – Andrew S Grove
    The go to handbook for implementation of management systems as you build a business
How Life Imitates Chess – Garry Kasparov
    Great insights from a superb mind on the difference between strategy and tactics when playing chess or in business
Influence – *The Psychology of Persuasion* – Robert Cialdini
    Ground breaking work on how we really take a decision to buy
Made to Stick – Chip and Dan Heath
    A look at the six factors that make information "sticky"
The Art of Learning - Josh Waitzkin

Fabulous insights into how to learn just about anything and get better at learning every day.

The Art of Thinking Clearly – Ralph Dobellie

An important guide on how to take decisions and review them

The Jelly Effect – Andy Bounds

Full of truths in terms of how we communicate and why we do it so badly so often.

The Strategy Book – Max McKeown

Great models on how to develop strategy as a business grows

Time to Think – Nancy Cline

The classic on how to find thinking space to take good decisions in the workplace

Tools of Titans – Tim Ferriss

The search for why successful people across many disciplines triumph

Winning! – Clive Woodward

A great story whilst sharing useful insights on how to improve team performance.

APPENDIX 10

Employee Engagement Research

Listed below are articles from the USA and UK relevant to employee engagement.

Full links to them online can be accessed at www. employeeengagementresources.net

Employee Engagement Research USA

1. An Empirical Study: Employee Engagement and Linkage to Organization Performance and Sustainability December 2018
2. Understanding Financially Stressed Millennials' Hesitancy to Seek Help: Implications for Organizations, 2018
3. Employee engagement: finding a generally accepted measurement scale 2018
4. Taking Dogs Into the Office: A Novel Strategy for Promoting Work Engagement, Commitment and Quality of Life May 2019
5. Definitional and Conceptual Muddling: Identifying the

the U.S. Federal Bureaucracy: A Self-Determination Theory Perspective 2014

Employee Engagement Research – UK

1. What Drives Employee Engagement in Different Global Contexts? A Comparison of the Enablers in the United Kingdom and India 2019
2. Employee engagement in discussion: Goals, perspectives and recommendations August 2017
3. Building work engagement: A systematic review and meta-analysis investigating the effectiveness of work engagement interventions 2016
4. Engaging with Employee Engagement in HRD Theory and Practice 2015
5. Engaging middle managers: Activities and resources which enhance middle manager engagement 2015
6. Exploring employee engagement with (corporate) social responsibility: A Social Exchange perspective on organisational participation 2014
7. The Effects of Perceived Corporate Social Responsibility on Employee Attitudes 2014
8. Work engagement as a mediator between employee attitudes and outcomes 2013

Additional Resources

1. Deloitte Employee Engagement Perspectives / Engaging the workforce (US - 2016)
2. Employee Job Satisfaction and Engagement: The Doors of Opportunity Are Open (US - 2017)
3. Deloitte Global Human Capital Trends (US - 2019)

4. Global Human Capital Trends 2019, Leading the social enterprise - Reinvent with a human focus. Trends in the United Kingdom - 2019
5. Unlocking the secrets of employee engagement - Deloitte United States - 2018
6. Employee Engagement on the Rise in the U.S. - 2018
7. Employee Engagement and Communication Research - U.S. - 2018
8. Case Study - Ricoh Workplace Transformation - U.K. - 2016

* * *

1. Impact of Service Climate and Psychological Capital on Employee Engagement: The Role of Organizational Hierarchy 2018
2. The Impact of Specialized Telephonic Guides on Employee Engagement in Corporate Well-Being Programs 2018
3. Building and sustaining work engagement – a participatory action intervention to increase work engagement in nursing staff 2017
4. Using online platforms to engage employees in unionism. The case of IBM 2017
5. Linking Empowering Leadership and Employee Creativity: The Influence of Psychological Empowerment, Intrinsic Motivation, and Creative Process Engagement 2017, American University of Maryland
6. Beyond feedback: introducing the 'engagement gap' in organizational energy management 2017
7. Peer communication improves environmental employee engagement programs: Evidence from a

quasi-experimental field study 2017

8. Employee voice: An antecedent to organisational engagement? 2017

9. Public relations and zones of engagement: Employees' lived experiences and the fundamental nature of employee engagement 2017

10. Investigating the incremental validity of employee engagement in the prediction of employee effectiveness: A meta-analytic path analysis 2016

11. Employee voice and work engagement: Macro, meso, and micro-level drivers of convergence? 2016

12. Demands or Resources? The Relationship Between HR Practices, Employee Engagement, and Emotional Exhaustion Within a Hybrid Model of Employment Relations 2015

13. Employee Engagement: Do Practitioners Care What Academics Have to Say – And Should They? 2015

14. A dialectical perspective on burnout and engagement 2015

15. Linking shifts in the national economy with changes in job satisfaction, employee engagement and work–life balance 2015

16. Antecedents of Organizational Engagement: Exploring Vision, Mood and Perceived Organizational Support with Emotional Intelligence as a Moderator 2014

Job Design Checklist

Aspect of Job	Considerations – Have you thought about the following?
Job Title	• Avoid abstract titles • Avoid use of gender pronouns • Use clear, concise language
Role Summary	• Avoid lengthy summary of duties • Focus on abilities required • Identify one or two key tasks of the role • Avoid language that could suggest bias, e.g. energetic candidates or dynamic candidates.

Hour of Work	• Consider what flexibility can be offered, e.g.
	  – Part time hours or job share
	  – Agile working hours
	  – Flexible start/finish times
	  – Alternative shift patterns
	• What if any overtime is required and for what reason?
	• Are any hours required to be worked outside 'normal' working time and what compensation is provided?

Location	• Consider where job can be carried out, e.g.
	  – At main office/site or alterative office/site
	  – Remote working from home or business hub
	• What if any travel is required – be specific to avoid excluding parents of young children or disabled candidates for whom travelling may be a challenge
	• Avoid requiring candidates to have a driving licence unless this can be justified. Could candidates use public/alternative transport to travel between sites if this is a requirement

Duties	• Avoid lengthy lists of duties that try to cover all eventualities • Focus on the key tasks that link to the role summary • Use descriptive language to outline performance indicators • When drafting duties consider what aids can be used to facilitate candidates with a disability
Experience	• Consider breadth of experience rather that setting a number of years. if specifying a set number of years can this be justified as it may rule out candidates • Consider transferrable skills gained through experience in alternative roles • Focus on the types of abilities that the role requires and that you are seeking candidates to have gained through work experience • Use relevant selection methods to test for relevant experience • Is training provided by the organisation? If so, then is relevant experience necessary? Looking for abilities may be more relevant than previous experience.

Qualifications	• Are there any legal/regulatory requirements that justify need for specific qualifications? • Avoid seeking candidates with 'contemporary' qualifications that could exclude older workers • Consider candidates educated outside NI and specify equivalents if you can justify need for qualifications • Consider alternatives to qualifications to include candidates who have opted for a vocational rather than academic route
Attributes	• Avoid general terms such as 'be a good team player' or 'have excellent communication skills' • Give specific examples of attributes required as they relate to the role, e.g. if report writing is a requirement of the role then specify this rather than 'good written communication skills' • Do not specify 'must speak English fluently' unless this can be justified • If specifying physical attributes, ensure these can be justified as they could exclude a large pool of candidates • Avoid using the term, 'physically fit' as again this is too general and could rule out a large pool of candidates • Focus on abilities that can be tested through selection methods.

Index

A page number followed by *qw* indicates a quick win. A page number followed by an *i* indicates an illustration.

**Matador**

For exclusive discounts on Matador titles,
sign up to our occasional newsletter at
troubador.co.uk/bookshop